Baedeker Amsterdam

Baedeker's

AMSTERDAM

Imprint

Cover picture: Boat Trip on the Canals

51 colour photographs
Map of Amsterdam, 16 plans and diagrams

Text:
Karin Reitzig, Amsterdam

Conception and editorial work:
Redaktionsbüro Harenberg, Schwerte
English language: Alec Court

Cartography:
Ingenieurbüro für Kartographie Huber & Oberländer, Munich
Hallwag AG, Bern (Map of Amsterdam)

General direction:
Dr Peter Baumgarten, Baedeker Stuttgart

English translation:
Babel Translations, Norwich

Source of illustrations:
Anthony (1), Diamond Center (2), Historia-Photo (3), Mauritius (3), Dutch Tourist Office (17), Prenzel (1), Vergeer (8), Rogge (8), Sperber (10)

Following the tradition established by Karl Baedeker in 1844, sights of particular interest and hotels and restaurants of particular quality are distinguished by one or two asterisks.

To make it easier to locate the various sights listed in the A–Z section of the guide, their coordinates on the large map of Amsterdam are shown in red at the head of each entry.

Only a selection of hotels, restaurants and shops can be given: no reflection is implied, therefore, on establishments not included.

In a time of rapid change it is difficult to ensure that all the information given is entirely accurate and up to date, and the possibility of error can never be entirely eliminated. Although the publishers can accept no responsibility for inaccuracies and omissions they are always grateful for corrections and suggestions for improvement.

US and Canadian edition
Prentice Hall Press

Licensed user:
Mairs Geographischer Verlag GmbH & Co., Ostfildern-Kemnat bei Stuttgart

Reproductions:
Gölz Repro-Service GmbH, Ludwigsburg

Printed in Great Britain by Jarrold & Sons Ltd Norwich

0 86145 119 8 UK

0–13–057969–6 US and Canada

3–87504–167–4 Germany

Contents

Preface

This Pocket Guide to Amsterdam is one of the new generation of Baedeker city guides.

Baedeker pocket-size guides, illustrated throughout in colour, are designed to meet the needs of the modern traveller. They are quick and easy to consult, with the principal features of interest described in alphabetical order and practical details about location, opening times, etc., shown in the margin.

Each guide is divided into three parts. The first part gives a general account of the city, its history, notable personalities and so on; in the second part the principal sights are described; and the third part contains a variety of practical information designed to help visitors to find their way about and make the most of their stay.

The new guides are abundantly illustrated and contain numbers of newly drawn plans. At the back of the book is a large city map, and each entry in the main part of the guide gives the coordinates of the square on the map in which the particular feature can be located. Users of this guide, therefore, will have no difficulty in finding what they want to see.

Facts and Figures

General Information

Capital

Amsterdam is the capital of the Netherlands, but the seat of government and the Queen's official residence are in The Hague.

Province

Amsterdam is in the Province of North Holland, in the NW of the country.

Geography

Its approximate latitude is 52° 50′ N and its longitude is 4° 53′ E. Below sea level, it lies above the deltas of the Rhine (or Rijn in Dutch) and the Meuse (or Maas) where the River Amstel flows into the IJ (pronounced "eye"), forming an inlet of the IJsselmeer.

Land Reclamation

The Dutch first rose to the challenge offered by their vast inland seas, whose beds could be 5 m (17 ft) and more below sea level, by using windmills to pump out four large lakes – Schermer, Beemster, Wormer and Purmer – in the 17th and 18th c. but it was not until the advent of steam power that they were able to tackle the Haarlemmermeer (Sea of Haarlem, 183 sq. km – 70 sq. miles) and the wide waters of the River IJ at Amsterdam.

The process of "droogmakerijen", literally of "making dry", is a simple one whereby the water has a dyke built around it then is pumped away via purpose-built "ring"canals. The clay of the former lake beds is extremely fertile and makes very good arable land, equalled only by the most recent of the Friesian polders, whereas reclaimed marshland can only be used for grazing.

Polders in the Zuider Zee

The greatest land reclamation project, made possible only by 20th c. technology, has been the poldering of the Zuider Zee (see Amsterdam A–Z, Zuider Zee), the vast inland sea formed by incursions of the North Sea in the Middle Ages. The narrow channel between North Holland and the island of Wieringen was closed off in 1924, and 1932 saw the completion of the "Afsluitdijk", the great dam that runs for 30 km (19 miles) between Wieringen and Friesland. Technically speaking, this was a gigantic undertaking because of the twice daily impact of the tides whereby the waters of the Zuider Zee exerted a progressively greater force within the narrowing confines of the dam advancing from both the NE and the SW.

With the completion of the Afsluitdijk, literally "the closing-off dyke", the Zuider Zee was a sea no longer and all that is left is the freshwater IJsselmeer. It is now relatively easy to fashion individual polders where the sea used to be, although this still entails a massive programme of all kinds of investment. The first stage was the drainage of the section between North Holland and the island of Wieringen (20,000 ha – 49,420 acres). The

◀ *Amsterdam: city of canals and bridges*

year 1942 saw the completion of the "Noordoostpolder", the NE polder (adjoining the Provinces of Friesland and Overijssel), and the first polder to be created in the Zuider Zee itself. The western part of the island fishing village of Urk was incorporated into the dyke. On the southern shore two polders have meanwhile been created. East Flevoland (54,000 ha – 133,434 acres) and South Flevoland (44,000 ha – 108,724 acres). A strip of open water has been left between the polders and the shore so that old coastal towns such as Elburg and Harderwijk still have access to the sea and the water table on the mainland can be maintained at an acceptable level. The last of the polders was to have been Markerwaard (40,000 ha – 98,840 acres) off the coast of North Holland and due for completion in 1980, but because of opposition by environmental groups the government has withdrawn the plan for

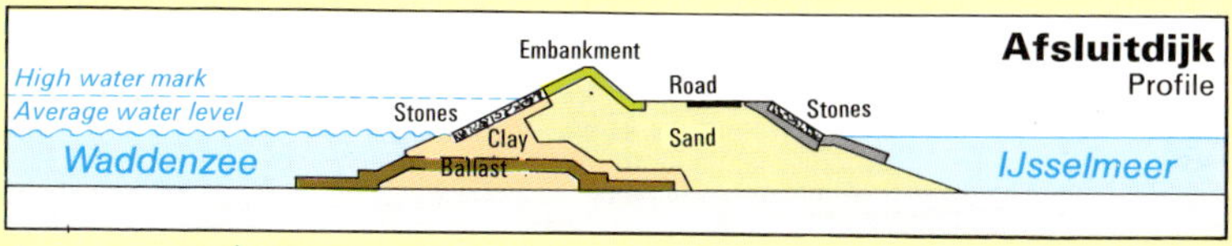

re-examination. This will still leave the IJsselmeer with a surface area of 110,000 ha (271,810 acres).

Deltaplan

Draining the Zuider Zee is, to date, the world's largest coastal land reclamation project. The Deltaplan, approved in 1957, was another such project and brought a merger of the islands of South Holland and Zeeland by closing off the open waters of the estuaries of the Rhine, Meuse and Scheldt; the construction of this dyke was completed in October 1986 (See Practical Information. Museums dealing with land reclamation).

Surface Area and Population

Amsterdam covers an area of 207 sq. km (80 sq. miles), 20 sq. km (8 sq. miles) of which is water, and, with about 700,000 inhabitants, is one of the main centres of the "Randstad Holland" (see p. 12). Its population is falling in numbers, however, since many Amsterdammers are moving out to elsewhere in the Randstad.

As a conurbation Amsterdam, with its associated townships of Amstelveen, Diemen, Haarlemmermeer, Haarlemmerliede and Spaarnwoude, Landsmeer, Oostzaan, Ouder-Amstel, Uithoorn, Weesp and Zaanstad, has a population of about a million.

The ancient nucleus of Amsterdam was Amstelredam, a 13th c. settlement on both banks of the Amstel. A grand project for

Zuider Zee, the world's largest land reclamation project to date

expansion was formulated in 1612, part of which was the famous "Three Canal Plan". This semicircular belt of three canals (*Gracht* means canal) – the Herengracht, Keizersgracht and Prinsengracht – took shape in the 17th c., with the Singelgracht as the outer ring. The concentrically laid-out canals are traversed by a number of radial canals and streets ending in squares, thus dividing the city into about 90 islands joined together by a thousand bridges and viaducts. The only exception to this arrangement is the Jordaan district in the NW of the city.

Around 1800 there were approximately 21,000 people (1981 *c.* 35,000) living within the encircling canals in an area of about 800 ha (about 1976 acres). Between 1870 and 1900 the population doubled from *c.* 255,000 to *c.* 510,000 and the area of the city increased to 1700 ha (4199 acres), spreading beyond the historical ring of canals and giving rise to the "Volksbuurten" or workers' districts of De Pijp, Kinkerbuurt and Dapperbuurt.

A general reconstruction plan (lasting until the year 2000) was embarked upon after the Second World War. In 1951 a start was made on building garden cities. The overall plan envisages the built-up zones taking shape like outspread fingers interspersed with greenbelt areas. The garden cities were, in the W (around Sloterplas, a 90 ha (222 acres) man-made lake), Slotermeer, Geuzenveld, Slotervaart, Osdrop and Overtoomse Veld; in the S, Buitenveldert; in the N, Nieuwendam, Noord, Buikslotermeer and Buiksloterbanne (nowadays districts of Amsterdam; see Districts p. 13); and in the SE, Bijlmermeer (now called Amsterdam Zuidoost).

Although these new residential districts considerably alleviated the catastrophic housing conditions in the overpopulated inner city, the housing shortage is still acute. Today approximately 700,000 people live in the city of Amsterdam in an area of *c.* 21,000 ha (51,810 acres) and there are currently 53,000 priority applications on the official housing waiting lists. A small section of Amsterdam residents have made a virtue of necessity and taken to the water, where they live in some 2800 houseboats moored along the canals.

Randstad Holland

Randstad Holland, where many of the citizens of Amsterdam now live, is the generic term used to decribe what has become a conurbation of townships encompassing the Dutch provinces of North Holland, South Holland and Utrecht. In the N it covers the area between the North Sea Canal zone and the southern shore of the IJsselmeer, and in the S between the Brielschen Meer, Alter Maas and Merwede. E to W it covers some 70 km (44 miles) and N to S it extends for 60 km (38 miles) and in that 3800 sq. km (1467 sq. miles) there live over 4 million people.

Randstad Holland can be regarded as having a N wing (covering Amsterdam, Haarlem, Haarlemmermeer, Zandvoort, Wormermeer, Zaanstad, Aalsmeer, Amstelveen, Weesp, Naarden, Bussum, Laren, Hilversum, Amersfoort Soest, Zeist, Maarssen, Vleuten-De-Meern and Utrecht) and a S wing (including The Hague, Katwijk, Wassenaar, Leiderdorp, Leiden, Leidschendam, Voorschoten, Voorburg, Rijswijk, Delft, Rozenburg, Vlaardingen, Schiedam, Krimpen aan den IJssel, Ridderkerk, Papendrecht, Dordrecht and Gorinchem).

Because of the concentration in this part of the country of industry, ports, commerce, administration and culture, as well

Houseboat: taking to the water because of the housing shortage

as intensive forms of agriculture, the Randstad Holland constitutes the economic heart of the Netherlands.

Districts

The city is divided up into 30 districts (Wijken). These are: Admiralenbuurt, Bijlmeer, Buikslotermeer, Buiksloterbanne, Buitenveldert, Centuur, Concertgebouw/Vondelpaarkbuurt, Driemond, De Eilanden, Geuzenveld, De Gouden Real, Indische Buurt, Jordaan, Landelijk Noord, Landlust/Bos en Lommer, Muiderpoort, Nieuwendam, Noord, Oostzaan, Osdorp, Oude Stad, Oud West, Rivierenbuurt, Sloten, Slotermeer, Slotervaart/Overtoomse Veld, Spaarndam, Staatslieden/Frederik-Hendrikbuurt, Watergraafsmeer, Zuid.

Administration

The city is administered by a City Council consisting of 36 Councillors and nine Aldermen, chaired by the Burgomaster (or Lord Mayor). The Councillors, who elect the Aldermen from among their own number, are elected by the people for a term of four years. The Burgomaster is appointed by the "Crown" (the Queen and the Council of Ministers) for a term of six years. The City Hall (Stadhuis), the seat of the City Council, is on the Oudezijds Voorburgwal.

People and Religion

People

The people of Amsterdam reflect the population structure of the Netherlands. Many of those who were forced to flee their own countries for political or religious reasons and took refuge in the Netherlands came to live in Amsterdam. The Netherlands, and

People in Amsterdam

with it Amsterdam, continues to attract many foreign workers as well as citizens of the former Dutch colonies who share the general belief that better living and working conditions are to be found in the mother country.
Thus among the people of Amsterdam one finds Indonesians (9600), Surinamese and people from the Dutch Antilles (together about 176,000 in the country as a whole) as well as Britons, Americans, Germans, Spaniards, Moroccans, Yugoslavs, Jews, Armenians and Levantines.

Religion

After the Reformation in the 16th c. there evolved in Amsterdam, alongside the Roman Catholic Church, many

Protestant sects such as the Evangelical Lutherans or the Amsterdam Reformed Church. The many refugees and other foreigners who settled in Amsterdam each brought their own faiths with them so that one finds a great many "imported" religions: there are Anglican and Presbyterian Churches and several synagogues, as well as places of worship for Buddhists, Hindus and Muslims.

Something of a general decline in the established religions has coincided with a flowering of "alternative" religious movements. Amsterdam is very much a centre for some of these such as Amitabh (the followers of the teachings of the Bhagwan Shree Rajneesh who formerly worked in Poona, India, as well as in the USA), the international society for Krishna Consciousness and Scientology.

The city has various yoga and meditation centres, of which the best-known are Kosmos, Stichting Universum and Mozeshuis (in the Moses and Aaron Church).

Communications

Port

Amsterdam's port and commerce are of considerable importance. The port on the S bank of the North Sea Canal has expanded in recent centuries with new port installations and industrial estates to cover an area of 2725 ha (6730 acres). Although it lags far behind Rotterdam in terms of tonnage, because of its location between the North Sea and the highly industrialised European hinterland, its significance as regards the trans-shipment of freight grew after the Second World War,

The busy port of Amsterdam

once the opening of the Amsterdam–Rhine Canal in 1952 brought it within easy reach of the European markets. The year 1876 had seen the opening of the North Sea Canal (270 m (886 ft) wide, 15 m (50 ft) deep and 15 km (9 miles) long) which provided a passage to the sea and was navigable irrespective of the state of the tide, thanks to the sluices at IJmuiden, part of the world's largest complex of sluices.

From the 17th c. onwards the port of Amsterdam looked after the country's traffic with its colonies overseas, and the decades following the Second World War have seen it grow into an industrial bulk-handling port. It has a container terminal and up-to-date storage facilities, with a petrochemical tank complex capable of taking over a million tonnes.

Every year several thousand ships are handled; the manufactured goods are destined for internal European markets, the raw materials for national and local industry.

Airport

Amsterdam's airport, Schiphol, which lies 10 km (6 miles) S of the city, is one of Europe's major airports. Over 60 airlines are represented, operating flights to more than 80 countries; on average Schiphol handles about 10 million passengers a year. Since 1986 the airport has been connected directly by rail (Centraal Station) with the centre of Amsterdam. Apart from its passenger traffic, Schiphol is an important distribution centre for valuable consumer goods, such as electronic equipment, and optical and medical instruments. Its annual freight turnover amounts to 300,000 tonnes.

Bikes – the Amsterdammer's favourite mode of transport

Rail and Underground

Through the international rail network Amsterdam is linked to all of Europe's major cities, with the volume of freight traffic matching the number of passengers.
To reduce the daily flow of cars in the rush-hour it is planned to extend the network of rail commuter services; and the Underground, with two routes and 20 stations, that came into operation in 1977 is one example of this. Public transport within the city is also catered for by buses and trams.

Arterial Roads

A1	Apeldoorn–Amersfoort
A2 (E8)	Utrecht–Arnhem
A4 (E10)	Schipol–The Hague–Rotterdam
A8	Zaandstad–Alkmaar–Afsluitdijk
A9	Amstelveen–Haarlem–Zandvoort
E35	Hilversum–Amersfoort
N5	Haarlem–Zandvoort

Bicycles

The bicycle is the most popular mode of transport (575,000 bikes among 700,000 residents), although it is never quite clear who owns which bike.

Culture

General

Amsterdam is the country's cultural centre and the main seat of learning and science (including the country's largest university and the Dutch Academy of Science), together with teaching and research. It is the home of world-famous museums such as the Rijksmuseum, with its great collection of old masters, the Stedelijk Museum for modern art and the Van Gogh Museum. The Concertgebouw and the Philharmonic Orchestras are internationally famous and the National Ballet and the Nederlands Dansk Theater are well known throughout the world. In 1986 the new opera house on Waterlooplein, Het Muziektheater, which is intended for operatic and ballet productions, was opened. It has a capacity for an audience of 1640.
Visitors come from all over the world to the Holland Festival every summer for its international programme of ballet, opera, music, theatre, folk-dance, etc.
Amsterdam also has many art galleries and innumerable avant-garde music, dance and drama groups. The most important newspaper and book publishers are located in Amsterdam.

Academies

Amsterdam's many academies include the Architectural Academy, the National Academy of the Visual Arts, the Gerrit Rietveld Academy (for industrial design), the Dutch Film Academy, the academies for the performing arts, etc.
Also in Amsterdam are the Royal Dutch Academy of Science, the Royal Society for the promotion of architecture, and the Royal Dutch Geographical Society.

Universities and Research Institutes

The University of Amsterdam, founded in 1877, now has about 30,000 students. The University has eight faculties and, with its institutes, laboratories and training colleges, is one of the most important in Europe.
In 1880 the Dutch Reformed Church set up its own university in Amsterdam. The "Free University", as it is called, has five faculties with about 13,000 students.

Concertgebouw Orkest: an orchestra with an international reputation

Amsterdam is famous for its diamond cutting

Also in Amsterdam one finds the Catholic Theological College, teacher training establishments, two conservatoires and a great many research institutes (including the State aviation and aerospace establishment, a nuclear physics research institute, the Royal Tropical Institute, the International Archive for Women's Movements, the International Institute for Social History and the Institute of Journalism).

Libraries

Among Amsterdam's major libraries are the University Library (*c.* 2 million volumes), the Public Library, the art libraries of the Stedelijk Museum and the Rijksmuseum, the Music Library and the library of the Tropical Museum.

Industry and Commerce

Centre of Dutch Commerce

As the capital of the Netherlands and Europe's second largest port, Amsterdam is important for its trade and commerce, and is the headquarters of about 16,000 businesses, and some 8% of the country's international trade passes through Amsterdam. It is also the centre of the country's car trade and most of the well-known makes of car have franchises here.
Amsterdam, in the 17th c. the greatest commercial city in the world, is today, with its concentration of major banks and insurance companies, central to Dutch business life. Its stock exchange, one of the oldest in the world, is of international standing. Besides the Bank of the Netherlands there are also foreign and private banks.
8% of the city's earnings come from tourism. It is the fourth largest tourist town in Europe.

Centre of Dutch industry

In addition to its port (see Amsterdam A–Z, Port) and commerce, Amsterdam also owes its importance in the economy to the fact that it lies in the middle of an industrial belt stretching from IJmuiden on the North Sea coast as far as Hilversum.
The industrial development of the port after the Second World War brought about a shift in emphasis from the traditional shipbuilding and repair with the coming, in the western part of the port, of a giant chemical and petrochemical complex on the completion of the pipeline to Rotterdam. With as many as 15,000 industrial companies in all located on the new industrial estates in the W, SW and S of the city, Amsterdam is the largest Dutch industrial city.
The major fields of production, besides the fast-growing chemical industry, are motor and aircraft manufacturing, together with various kinds of engineering.
Amsterdam's diamond industry enjoys worldwide renown and was brought here by the diamond-cutters who fled the sacking of Antwerp in 1586. It is also the centre for the manufacture of wooden and leather goods, soap-making (one of its oldest trades) and the film industry.
Amsterdam has also long been the centre of the Dutch textile industry, leading the way in fashion and ready-to-wear clothing, and it is also an important producer of foodstuffs, confectionery and similar luxury products, with chocolate and cigarette factories, breweries, etc.
A large number of printing works points to the city's importance as the focus for the Dutch press, publishing and the book trade.

Famous People

Karel Appel
(b. 25.4.1921)

Karel Appel, who was born in Amsterdam, is one of the most internationally famous and controversial post-war Dutch painters. He received his first major commission in 1949 – a frieze for Amsterdam City Hall entitled "Vragende Kinderen" ("Questioning Children") – which sparked off such a public outcry that the work had to be covered up for a time.
In 1950 Appel settled in Paris where he joined the international experimental school and was one of the founders of the COBRA group (Copenhagen, Brussels, Amsterdam) composed of artists now enjoying international acclaim such as Corneille, Constant, Alechinsky, Asger Jorn and Lucebert.
In the fifties Appel took part in many important exhibitions and received international awards and prizes, including the 1954 UNESCO Prize at the Venice Biennale and the Guggenheim Prize in 1960.
Karel Appel's work, much of which can be seen in the Stedelijk Museum, is characterised by an especially expressive and vibrant use of colour.

Hendrik Petrus Berlage
(21.2.1856–12.8.1934)

Hendrik Petrus Berlage was a brilliant and typically Dutch architect whose highly original style in the building that made him famous, the Amsterdam Exchange (begun 1897), marked the transition between historicism and the 20th c. A great influence on architecture both inside and outside the Netherlands, he was also responsible for the bridge over the Amstel bearing his name and the Gemeentelijk (Municipal) Museum in The Hague, while the furniture he designed assured him a prominent place in the field of applied arts.

Anne Frank
(2.6.1929–March 1945)

Anne Frank, a Jewish girl from Germany, achieved fame through her diary which has been filmed and translated into many languages.
The Jewish Frank family fled Hitler's Frankfurt in 1933 and came to Amsterdam where they went into hiding during the German occupation. Anne kept a diary on their life over this period (12 June 1942–1 August 1944) which ended when the whole family was discovered and transported to Germany. Anne, together with her mother and sister, died in Belsen concentration camp and only her father survived. After the Liberation the diary was found in the family's Amsterdam hideout and published.

Rembrandt
(Harmensz van Rijn)
(15.7.1606–4.10.1669)

Rembrandt, the most famous of all Dutch painters, moved to Amsterdam in 1632, after an early creative period in his native Leyden; in 1634 he married Saskia van Uijlenburgh, the wealthy daughter of a burgomaster. In 1639 he bought the house in the Jodenbreestraat which is today the Rembrandthuis.
During his first ten years in Amsterdam he was much in demand for his portraits, and almost two-thirds of all his commissioned work dates from this period. His portraits were true to life and made no concessions to flattery. Besides his impressive individual portraits (including Burgomaster J. Six), his group

Joost van den Vondel

Rembrandt

portraits ("The Anatomy Lesson of Dr Tulp") and self-portraits (with Saskia, the painter as the Prodigal Son), he also painted biblical themes and, later in life, landscapes.

As Rembrandt increasingly declined to subjugate the artistic integrity of his portraits to the wishes of his patrons, the number of commissions declined, and, in fact, the patrons who commissioned "The Night Watch" refused to accept it.

After Saskia's death in 1642 Rembrandt got into personal and financial difficulties and in 1656 was declared bankrupt. Titus, his son by Saskia, and Hendrickje Stoffels, his common-law wife, formed a company to help Rembrandt's financial situation but until his death he remained encumbered by debts, in growing artistic and social isolation (Rembrandt's "The Swearing-in of the Batavians under Julius Civilis" for the new Town Hall in Amsterdam was rejected and replaced by the work of one of his pupils).

When he died in 1669 Rembrandt was buried outside the Westerkerk and was only subsequently reinterred inside the church.

Rembrandt left 562 paintings, 300 etchings and 1600 drawings. His best-known works are "The Night Watch" (1642), "The Anatomy Lesson on Dr Tulp" (1632), "The Staalmeesters" (1661/2) and "The Jewish Bride" (*c.* 1665), all of which are in the Rijksmuseum. His best-known self-portrait hangs in the Mauritshuis in The Hague, and almost all his etchings and many of his drawings can be seen in the Rembrandthuis.

Baruch (Benedictus) de Spinoza (24.11.1632–21.2.1677)

The Dutch philosopher Baruch (or Benedictus) de Spinoza was born in the Jewish quarter of Amsterdam and given a Hebrew education. His independent thinking ran counter to Jewish beliefs and led in 1656 to his excommunication. A considerable influence on Western philosophy, he was above all a rationalist and set out to prove his metaphysical pantheistic doctrines by mathematical demonstration.

His best-known work, "Ethics demonstrated by geometrical methods", written between 1660 and 1675, was not published until after his death.

Spinoza's house in The Hague was taken over by the Spinoza Institute in 1927.

Joost van den Vondel (17.11.1587–5.2.1679)

Joost van den Vondel was the greatest poet of the Dutch Renaissance. His writings ranged from satirical, historical, patriotic and religious poetry to his 32 plays, of which the best-known are "Gijsbreght van Aemstel" (1637) and "Lucifer" (1654). He also translated the Psalms, Ovid and Virgil into Dutch.
Van den Vondel, who played an active part in the political and religious struggles of his times and was converted to Catholicism in 1641, died aged 92 in Amsterdam in 1679. The city's largest park is named after him.

History of the City

1270 — A dam is built separating the mouth of the Amstel from the arm of the Zuider Zee called the "IJ".

1275 — Floris V, Count of Holland, grants the people of the fishing village of Amstelledamme freedom from tolls on travel and on trade in their own goods within the County of Holland.

1300 — Amsterdam receives its charter.

1317 — The Bishops of Utrecht transfer the city to Count Willem III of Holland.

1323 — The city becomes the point where duty is levied on beer imported from Hamburg, thus leading to increased trade with the Hanseatic towns.

1345 — The "miracle of the Host" makes Amsterdam a place of pilgrimage, and pilgrims flock to the chapel built in the Kalverstraat in 1347. When Emperor Maximilian is cured of an illness while on a pilgrimage in 1489 he grants the city the right to bear the Imperial crown in its coat of arms.

from 1400 — The four Burgomasters are elected annually by the Council of Elders which gives the city relative independence from the country's rulers.

1421 — The city of Amsterdam is almost completely destroyed by a great fire.

1481 — Building of a stone city wall.

1535 — The city is plunged into the upheaval of the Reformation. Anabaptists run naked in a state of religious ecstasy over the Dam and almost succeed, on 10 May, in occupying the Town Hall. The city fathers summon the aid of the Hapsburg Emperor Charles V.

1538 — The population of Amsterdam has grown to over 30,000.

1566 — During a famine churches and monasteries are stormed by adherents of the Reformation. Philip II of Spain succeeds to the throne of Charles V.

1567 — Duke of Alba occupies Amsterdam on behalf of Philip II and savagely persecutes the followers of the Reformation.

During an uprising by the Northern Provinces of the Low Countries Amsterdam remains pro-Spanish.	1568
William the Silent, Prince of Orange, becomes the leader of the uprising against Spain.	1572
After the city surrenders to William's troops, Amsterdam joins in the Dutch War of Independence from Spain. All pro-Spanish civic leaders, clerics and clergy have to leave the city ("Alteratie"). A new civic administration consists mainly of immigrant Reformed merchants. The "Satisfactie van Amsterdam" lays down that no one may be persecuted for their beliefs.	1578
Amsterdam becomes one of the most important cities for commerce in the world, a centre for culture and science, a city with flourishing crafts and a cosmopolitan population. Refugees from the whole of Europe come to settle in the city.	1578 onwards
A fleet, financed mainly by Amsterdam merchants, succeeds in finding a sea route to India round the southern tip of Africa.	1595–1597
Founding of the United East India Trading Company, with Amsterdam merchants among the major shareholders.	1602
Founding of the Stocks and Commodities Exchange.	1611
The three canals (Herengracht, Keizersgracht and Prinsengracht) are built as part of the fourth project to extend the city, with the workers' district of the Jordaan in the W.	1613
The city's population reaches 100,000.	1620
The "Golden Age" of Amsterdam, when Amsterdam becomes the most important port in the world.	17th c.
War with England. Amsterdam loses its supremacy at sea.	1780–1784
End of the rule of a number of Amsterdam families. Promulgation of the principles of the French Revolution.	19 January 1795
The Low Countries become the Republic of Batavia.	1795–1806
Amsterdam becomes the capital of the Kingdom of the Netherlands under Louis Napoleon.	1806
The Netherlands are made part of France. The Continental Blockade, which cuts the city off from its traditional markets, finally ends Amsterdam's position as chief trading city.	1810
After the defeat of Napoleon and expulsion of the French, Amsterdam becomes the capital of the Kingdom of the Netherlands, a constitutional monarchy under William I, although the seat of government is in The Hague.	1813
A railway line is built to Haarlem.	1839
A direct link with the sea is established with the construction of the North Sea Canal. New prosperity for the port.	1876

History of the City

1913	Social Democrats win a majority on the City Council and Amsterdam is henceforward a stronghold of democratic socialism.
1914–1918	The Netherlands stay neutral during the First World War. Amsterdam is plunged into a series of crises during this time (unemployment, food shortages, influx of refugees).
1920	Amsterdam has a population of 647,000.
16 May 1940	German troops occupy the city. Deportation of Jews is begun.
25 February 1941	The "February Strike" is organised by the workers of Amsterdam in protest against the deportation of their Jewish fellow citizens.
1940–1945	Although the resistance movement is particularly strong in Amsterdam (underground press, direct action against the forces of occupation), by the end of the war approximately 100,000 Jews have been deported and Amsterdam's Jewish community has been almost completely eliminated.
5 May 1945	The city is liberated by Canadian troops.
1952	Opening of the Amsterdam–Rhine Canal.
1964–1966	Appearance of the anti-Establishment "Provos".
10 March 1966	Mass demonstrations triggered off by the wedding of Princess Beatrix and Claus von Amsberg lead to the subsequent dismissal of the Burgomaster and Chief of Police.
1970	The "Kabouter" (Gnome Party), successors to the Provos, win five seats on the City Council.
1975	Amsterdam celebrates its 700th anniversary; clashes between the residents of the Nieuwmarkt district and the police. Attempts to prevent demolition of housing to make way for the Underground.
1979	Over 60,000 on Amsterdam's housing waiting list. Many empty houses occupied by the "Krakers".
30 April 1980	Abdication of Queen Juliana. Queen Beatrix pledges her oath of allegiance to the constitution. Coronation of Queen Beatrix in the Nieuwe Kerk. Riots around the church and palace, away from the heavily protected route of the procession, are directed not so much at the Queen as at the acute housing shortage in Amsterdam.
1981	Law for the registration of empty dwellings. Illegal occupation of premises prohibited.
1985	Amsterdam applies to stage the Olympic Games in 1992.
1986	Amsterdam celebrates its 400th centenary as a diamond centre. Opening of the new Opera House "Het Musiektheater" on Waterlooplein.

Amsterdam A–Z

*Aalsmeer

The district of Aalsmeer (Province of North Holland) on the canal around the Haarlemmermeer polder is part of the Randstad Holland (see General Information, Randstad Holland). Over one third of its area is covered by lakes, the "Westeinderplassen". It is internationally famous for its flower auctions, which are the largest in Europe.

In the Middle Ages Aalsmeer owed its importance to peat, to fishing and cattle breeding but since about 1450, with the growth of nearby Amsterdam and the 19th c. draining of the Haarlemmermeer, it has become increasingly given over to horticulture.

The flower-growing began with lilac; later the emphasis shifted to pot plants and cut flowers. Today Aalsmeer has over 600 flower-growers, their glass-houses cover an area of 600 hectares (1482 acres) and the annual turnover from the auctions is 380 million guilders.

The flowers are despatched throughout Europe via Schiphol airport (see entry).

There are daily auctions of cut flowers, as well as auctions of pot plants which are held from Monday to Friday between 7.30 and 11 a.m.

Buses
Stop opposite the Central Station; CN 171, 172

Location
12 km (8 miles) SW

VVV
See Practical Information, Information

Aalsmeer's flower auctions are among the most famous in the world

Auctions
Legmeerdijk 313

The auction building has a visitors' gallery where the interested observer can hear a commentary on the auction procedure in any one of seven languages and watch what is going on.
Every year on the first Saturday in September there is a flower parade from Aalsmeer to Amsterdam and back, and this is well worth seeing.

Achterburgwal (officially: Oudezijds- and Nieuwezijds Achterburgwal) B/C2/3

Buses
22, 46, 55, 56

The Nieuwezijds Achterburgwal was dug as a canal in 1380 when the town was being developed and extended from the Spui, the original city boundary, to the Hekelfeld. The canal was filled in in 1867, much to the annoyance of some of the shopkeepers in the Kalverstraat (see entry) who were afraid that the resultant Spuistraat would become a shopping street in competition with their own.
Their worries were unfounded because Spuistraat has mainly become a street of offices.
The Oudezijds Achterburgwal was excavated in about 1385 behind the Oudezijds Voorburgwal as a second defensive canal, and stretches from the Grimburgwal to the Zeedijk. It is the narrowest Burgwal and used to be one of the "better" residential areas. Proof of this is the inscription "Fluweelenburgwal" on the gables of the Driegrachtenhuis (the "House on the three canals" where Grimburgwal, O.Z. Voorburgwal and O.Z. Achterburgwal meet) which alludes to the fact that the prominent citizens of the 17th c. dressed in silk and satin.
House No. 47, among others, is worth seeing. Nowadays the property of the Salvation Army, it used to be the house of the Lieutenant in Rembrandt's painting "The Night Watch".
A little to the SW of the Achterburgwal is the Museum Amstelkring (see entry) which houses a collection of ecclesiastical antiquities, pictures and copperplate engravings.

Albert Cuypmarkt H7

Location
Albert Cuypstraat, in the S of the city centre

Trams
4, 5, 16, 24, 25

Times of opening
Daily (except Sun.)

The Albert Cuypmarkt has nearly 400 stalls and sells almost everything needed in the kitchen or the home: butter, eggs, cheese, fish, poultry, local and exotic fruits and vegetables, spices, tea, cakes, biscuits, fabrics, wool, haberdashery, pots and pans and cutlery, clothes (new and second-hand), and thousands of odds and ends, some useful, some not. Between van Woustraat and Ferdinand Bolstraat you can stroll at your leisure (although it gets rather crowded on Saturday mornings) and savour the smells of fresh fruit and fish, watch the people around you, listen to the cries of the stall-holders, test the quality of the goods on offer, simply look around or even pick up a bargain.
Those wanting to fortify themselves with coffee and rolls would do well to try the café "De Markt" where the stall-holders warm themselves at simple tables in surroundings looking almost the same as when the market first started 75 years ago.

Alkmaar: famous for its cheese market

*Alkmaar

Rail
From Central Station
(3 times per hour)

Location
37 km (23 miles) NW (A9)

VVV
See Practical Information, Information

Alkmaar's number one tourist attraction is its cheese market, held, strictly in accordance with tradition, between 10 and 12 every Friday morning from mid-April to mid-September in front of the weigh-house. The cheese-porters are dressed in white and wear hats bearing the colours of the guild. They carry the cheeses (sometimes 80 Edam cheeses at a time!) on litters, have them weighed on the scales and load them on to carts. (In fact all this is just for show; the actual cheese market is held in the exchange.)

Alkmaar is the ancient centre of North Holland. It lies 8 km (5 miles) from the North Sea coast on the North Holland canal (in the Province of North Holland). Today its major industries are metals, paper, cocoa and carpets.

The town received its charter from Count William II in 1254. In 1517 it fell victim to plundering by a band led by "Big Piet". Alkmaar played a special role in the Dutch struggle for independence from the Spanish by being the first to succeed in routing the son of the Duke of Alba, Frederick of Toledo, who was besieging the town. This took place on 8 October 1573 when the sluices were opened and the surrounding area was flooded.

Alkmaar flourished after the war of independence, owing partly to local land reclamation. Wars of religion raged in the town between 1609 and 1621 but after the lifting of the siege by the French (1810–13), Alkmaar, as an inland town, enjoyed a more peaceful fate than the towns on the Zuider Zee.

Times of opening
Mon.–Fri. 9 a.m.–noon, 2–5 p.m.

Times of opening
1 Apr.–31 Oct. Mon.–Thurs. & Sat. 10 a.m.–4 p.m., Fri. 9 a.m.–4 p.m.

Times of opening
Mon.–Thurs. 10 a.m.–noon, 2–5 p.m., Fri. 10 a.m.–5 p.m., Sun. 2–5 p.m.

Alkmaar's impressive townscape, with its many 16th–18th c. historic buildings, guild-houses and patrician homes, has been preserved intact. The finest and most important historic buildings include:
The Grote Kerk (St Laurenskerk, Kerkplein), built 1470–1516, a late-Gothic cruciform basilica with a famous organ (1645) by Jacob van Campen.
The Stadhuis (town hall, Langestraat), dating from 1520 with its late-Gothic front gable.
The weigh-house, converted in 1582 from the former Church of the Holy Ghost, with a beautiful tower added in 1599. It houses a cheese museum.
The Municipal Museum (Stedelijk Museum. Doerenstraat 3), with its very interesting toy collection. (Admission free)

Amsterdamse Bos (Amsterdam Wood)

Location
Nieuwe Kalfjeslaan
Amstelveen

Museum
Koenenhade

Bus
70

Times of opening
9 a.m.–5 p.m.

The Amsterdam wood was created in 1934 during the Depression as the result of a "job-creation scheme" which was to guarantee work for 1000 men for five years. In the 900 ha (over 2000 acres) area on the SW edge of the city can be found about 150 species of trees from all parts of the world, in addition to shrubs and trees native to the Netherlands. Animal life is just as varied; more than 200 species of birds find their home here.
The Bos Museum is both an information centre for the leisure opportunites to be found in the Amsterdamse Bos and at the same time a museum concerned with the development of the woodland up to the present day. For children there is a diorama with stuffed animals.
The wood is very popular with the people of Amsterdam and offers many sporting facilities, including riding, walking, cycling, jogging, fishing swimming, rowing and sailing as well as restaurants and cafés.
Anyone wishing to stay longer here can make use of the camp site (see Practical Information, Camp Sites).

*Amsterdams Historisch Museum A3

Entrances
Kalverstraat 92
Sint Luciensteeg 27
Gedempte Begijnensloot
Begijnhof

Trams
1, 2, 4, 5, 9, 16, 24, 25

Times of opening
Tues.–Sat. 10 a.m.–5 p.m.
Sun. and public holidays 1–5 p.m.

Admission fee

Telephone
25 58 22

This museum has been housed in the former municipal orphanage on the St Luciensteeg since 1975, when Amsterdam celebrated its 700th anniversary. The name Luciensteeg harks back to the monastery of St Lucia founded in 1414 which, besides a chapel and a brewery, also had a farm (today restaurant and museum). After the dissolution of the monastery this was the municipal orphanage from 1578 to 1960.
Today the restored buildings 1963–1975 surrounding spacious courtyards are set out as a museum which uses modern methods to illustrate the past. The visitor can learn about the constantly changing position of Amsterdam in the country and in the world, the growth of the city and the port and the life of its citizens on its streets and in the home. The exhibits range from prehistoric finds and the town's original charter, to items from the present day. Reclamation of the land from the sea is explained by means of slides. Special exhibitions illustrate particular aspects of Amsterdam's varied history.

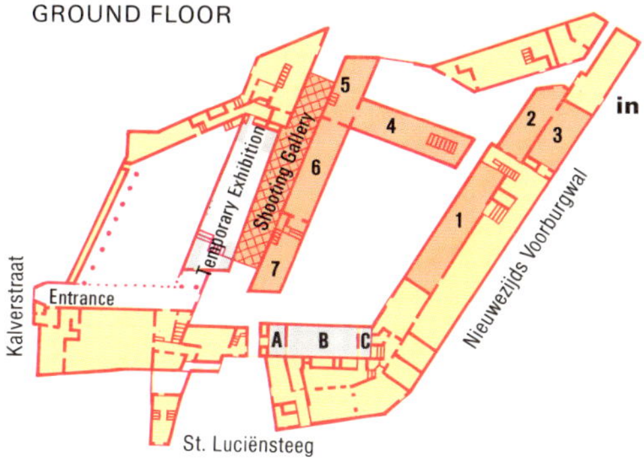

Amsterdams Historisch Museum

in the former municipal orphanage

- A Geldkamer
  History of the buildings
- B Regentenkamer
  Historic chamber (restored)
- C Van Speykkamer
  Mementoes of the national hero J. C. J. van Speyk (1802–31)
- D Library
  History of the city
- E Print department
  Temporary exhibitions

GROUND FLOOR

1 In the course of time
Historical development of the city, occupations, customs, architecture

2 Origins of the city
First mention in 13th c.; contemporary illustrations

3 Commerce/pilgrimage
Founding of monasteries; Baltic trade; merchants' portraits; pilgrims' insignia

4 Growth and development
16th c.: trading post for grain, textiles, timber, wine. Consequences of Reformation and 80 Years War; iconoclasm

5 On the world's seas
Voyages around Africa, to the West Indies and South America; seascapes; overseas trading companies; science and cartography

6 Powerful city
Town planning and commercial prosperity in 17th and 18th c.; dominance in the Republic of the United Netherlands

7 Guns and butter
Capital market ("the banker of Europe"); wars with France and England
Late 18th–early 19th c.: symptoms of decline

UPPER FLOOR

8 Work through trade
Stock exchange, guilds, workers

9 Life in Amsterdam
Development in 16th and 17th c. Construction of canals and islands

10 Religious freedom
Catholic Church loses its hegemony late 16th c.; building of reformed churches in 17th c.

10a Archaeological finds

11 Rich and poor
Late 16th c. society; crime and punishment, law, reform

12 "Golden" age
Cultural heyday in the 17th c.: painting, architecture, printing, gold- and silverware

13–14 Developments in the arts
18th c. refinement: painting, portraiture, printing, furniture, clocks, tableware

15 Science/pleasure
Educational establishments in 18th and 19th c.; Athenaeum as forerunner of the university; coffee houses and other meeting places

16/1 "Velvet" revolution
Political and economic decline in 18th c.; French invasion 1795; Napoleon's rule; Batavian Republic

16/2 City of the Netherlands
Proclamation of the Kingdom of the Netherlands 1813; poverty and unemployment; revitalisation of trade after 1830; improvement in living conditions after 1870; construction of railways and canals; founding of political parties

17 Lead-in to the present day
City development in the early 20th c.; isolation in the First World War; economic stagnation in the 1920s; construction of airport, 1926; Social Democracy most powerful force in the city; radicalisation in the 1930s; Amsterdam in the Second World War; persecution of the Jews

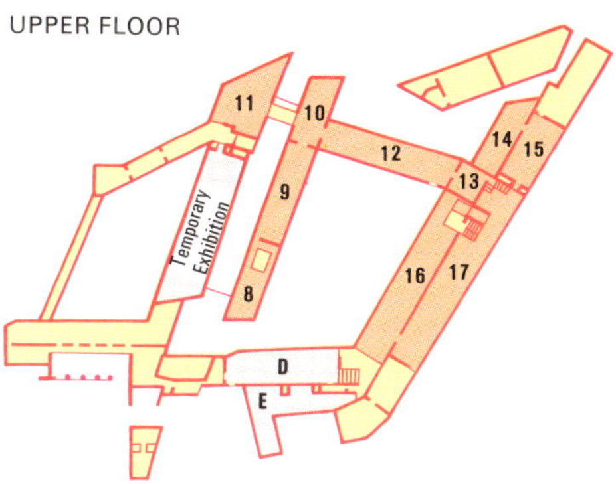

Historical Museum: entrance and A. J. Vinckenbrinck's "David and Goliath"

There is easy access to the inner courtyards, the shooting gallery, the audio-visual programmes (in English and Dutch) on the history of the building and the restaurant during museum opening hours.
The library possesses a rich collection of literature on the history of the city. In addition graphics, drawings and the Fodor Bequest can be inspected by arrangement. The library is open from Tuesday to Saturday.

Anne Frank Huis (House of Anne Frank) H5

Location
Prinsengracht 263

Buses
21, 67

Trams
13, 17

Times of opening
Mon.–Sat. 9 a.m.–5 p.m., Sun. and public holidays 10 a.m.–5 p.m.

Closed
1 Jan., Yom Kippur

Admission fee

In this house on the Prinsengracht the Frank family, Jewish refugees from Frankfurt, hid from the Germans with a few friends between 1942 and 1944. Here Anne Frank wrote her famous diary, which has been translated into 51 languages. The final entry is for 1 August 1944. On 4 August they were arrested and sent to concentration camps. Only Anne's father, Otto Frank, survived; Anne herself died in Bergen-Belsen two months before the end of the war.
In 1957 the house was given by its owner to the Anne Frank foundation. The foundation had it restored and turned it into a meeting-place for young people of all nationalities. The front part of the house contains exhibitions of material documenting the persecution of the Jews under the Third Reich and publications on neo-Nazi movements the world over. The back of the house, where the Frank family had their hiding-place, has been kept as far as possible in its original state.

Artis (officially: Zoo Natura Artis Magistra) J/K6

Amsterdam Zoo was set up by a private association calling itself Natura Artis Magistra (Nature is the instructor of Art), from which the zoo got its name. The aim was to give the townspeople a better understanding of the world of nature by means of exhibits and live animals. In 1838 a site was acquired in the Plantage Middenlaan and the zoo that was built there came to be known as Artis, an abbreviation of the Latin name. There were few animals to start with but their numbers soon grew, for example by purchases from travelling menageries. In its first hundred years the zoo was open only to members of the Association who came here for Sunday walks and attended the concerts held here in the summer months.

When the Association got into financial difficulties the city of Amsterdam and the Province of North Holland bought the zoo and rented it to the Association for the nominal annual sum of one guilder in 1937, since when the zoo has been open to the public.

Right from the start the layout has been continuously extended and modernised. Most animals live in outdoor enclosures corresponding as closely as possible to their natural habitats. The zoo's main attractions are the aquarium – which, with about 700 species of fish, is the second largest collection in the world (after West Berlin) – and the nocturnal animal house. Children find the children's farm especially interesting.

The zoo has a very interesting Zoological Museum attached. (See Practical Information, Museums).

Location
Plantage Kerklaan 30–40

Bus
56

Tram
9

Times of opening
1 Apr.–30 Sept.: daily
9 a.m.–6 p.m.
1 Oct.–31 March: daily
9 a.m.–5 p.m.

Admission fee

Artis: Amsterdam's zoo is a children's paradise

Begijnhof: an idyllic spot in the centre of the city

Centraal Station: Amsterdam's central station

* Begijnhof (Beguine convent) — A3

The Begijnhof is a tiny idyllic spot in the centre of the city where nowadays elderly ladies without families and young women students live for a very low rent. The green lawn of the courtyard is surrounded by houses which include some of the oldest in Amsterdam, among them the only remaining wooden house in the city.

In 1346 the buildings, which at that time still lay outside the city boundaries, were endowed for pious Catholic girls (begijnen) who wanted to live in a religious community but not in the seclusion of a convent. They devoted themselves to the care of the poor and sick. In a "Begijnhof" they were not called upon to abandon their personal freedom and could leave whenever they wished. They had their own accommodation and were not required to renounce personal possessions.

When Amsterdam went over to Protestantism the "begijnen" had to make their church over to the English Presbyterian community and hold their services in secret in a small chapel opposite the church. The Begijnhof was turned into almshouses but the "begijnen" retained the right to be buried in their "old" church. The last "begijn" died in 1971.

Location
Gedempte Begijnensloot (entrance in Spui)

Trams
1, 2, 4, 5g, 9, 16, 24, 25

Bloemenmarkt (Flower market) — A2/3

The flower market on the Singel (see entry) is a Mecca for anyone in search of trees, shrubs, plants, flowers or herbs for the home, garden or balcony. Cut flowers and pot plants of every variety, even palms as tall as a man, are offered for sale on the street and on the boats, the whole scene looking like a colourful garden. It is also possible to buy everything imaginable for the garden, such as peat, soil, fertiliser, seeds, tools, watering cans and plant pots.

The flower market has not always been on the Singel; in the 17th c. it was held every Monday in the summer in St Luciensteeg, near the present-day Historical Museum. It must have had a huge selection to offer then, too, since one contemporary complained that it was difficult and tiresome to list the names of the shrubs and plants on sale.

Location
Singel

Trams
1, 2, 4, 5, 9, 16, 24, 25

Times of opening
Mon.–Sat. 9 a.m.–5 p.m.

Centraal Station (Central station) — H/J5(C1)

More than 1000 trains, including 50 international trains, travel in and out of Amsterdam's central station every day. Its architect was P. J. H. Cuypers (also the architect of the Rijksmuseum – see entry) and it was built on three artificial islands and 8687 piles. On the N side of the station (de Ruijterkade), facing the harbour, are the moorings of numerous motor-boats and ferries. The need for the station became apparent when in 1860 Amsterdam was linked to Alkmaar and Den Helder to the N. The public joined in its opening in 1889 with considerable enthusiasm and bought as many as 14,000 platform tickets for the occasion.

The station building, which has an especially interesting Art Nouveau first-class waiting-room, also received international attention, and when in 1900 the Japanese were looking for a model for Tokyo station they opted for Amsterdam.

Location
De Ruijterkade

Buses
18, 21, 22, 28, 29, 32, 33, 34, 35, 39, 47, 49, 56, 57

Trams
1, 2, 4, 5, 9, 13, 16, 17, 24, 25

Metro

Concertgebouw G7

Location
Van Baerlestraat 98

Telephone
71 83 45

Trams
2, 5, 16

The building of Holland's most famous concert hall was inspired by a German. In 1879 Johannes Brahms was invited to Amsterdam to conduct his Third Symphony. After the concert Brahms said: "You are good people but bad musicians!" The people of Amsterdam took this harsh criticism to heart and formed a society to establish an orchestra and a concert hall that would seat about 2000. The concert hall was designed by A. van Gendt and inaugurated in 1888. The 65-member orchestra was entrusted to Willem Kes who laid the foundations for the fine reputation both of the orchestra and of the concert hall. Kes's successor was the 24-year-old Willem Mengelberg who was associated with the Concertgebouw Orchestra for 50 years. Under his direction it developed into one of the best orchestras in the world. He introduced the symphonic music of Mahler and of Richard Strauss who dedicated his "Heldenleben" to Mengelberg. The 1920 Mahler music festival became a high point in the history of the concert hall. The composers Reger, Debussy, Ravel, Hindemith, Milhaud and Stravinsky were guest conductors of their own works in the concert hall.

Today more than 500 concerts take place annually, and the outstanding acoustic properties of the hall are still renowned. However, the building was threatening to sink into the marshy ground on which the city stands. Over £12 million was spent to ensure its safety, work which was concluded in 1985.

Dam with Nationaal Monument (National Monument) B2

Trams
4, 9, 16, 24, 25

The Dam, with the Royal Palace (see Koninklijk Paleis) and the national monument, is no longer either geographically or administratively the centre of Amsterdam, but has remained the heart of the city. It was the Dam which gave the city its name: built about 1270, it separated the Amstel from the IJ (an arm of the Zuider Zee – see entry). Amsterdam's history began here with the founding of the original settlement trading in fish and cattle. As in the past, the people of Amsterdam still assemble on the Dam for official events.

In its early days a small market grew up on the square known, in accordance with medieval custom, as the "Plaetse", and today the square still retains its market character.

Nationaal Monument (National Monument)

The National Monument, a 22 m (72 ft) high obelisk, was erected on the Dam after the Second World War. This memorial to the victims of the war and monument to the Liberation and peace was designed by J. J. P. Oud and decorated with sculptures by J. W. Rädeler symbolising, among other things, War (four male figures), Peace (woman and child) and Resistance (two men with howling dogs).

Embedded in the obelisk are urns containing earth from the eleven provinces. A twelfth urn contains earth from the cemetery of honour in Indonesia. Since Flevoland has been the twelfth Dutch province since 1986, another urn will probably be added.

The national monument on the Dam

The monument was dedicated by Queen Juliana on 4 May 1956, the national day of remembrance, and since then the Dutch Queen and her consort have laid wreaths here every year on that day. A two-minute silence is observed throughout the Netherlands at 8 o'clock that same evening.
The rest of the year the Liberation monument is a place where young people from all over the world meet.

*Delft

Rail
From Centraal Station

Location
60 km (37 miles) SW (A4, A13)

VVV
See Practical Information, Information

Delft, with its picturesque old city centre encircled by canals, is well worth a visit. This town of princes on the River Schie in the Province of South Holland is famous for its blue and white earthenware ("delftware") and for its annual art and antiques fair.
Delft received its charter in 1246 and from the 13th c. onwards brewing and carpet-making played important roles. Prince William of Orange (William the Silent) made Delft his seat in 1580. Owing mainly to its earthenware the town reached the peak of its prosperity in the 17th c. when it had 30 tile potteries (1650–1760), but by 1854 only the Royal Delft China Factory "De Porceleyne Fles" remained, and this won a new claim to fame as the manufacturer of Delft-blue china (Rotterdamse Weg 196, can be visited).
A tour of the town should include the following historical buildings:

Times of opening
Apr.–Sept.: Mon.–Sat. noon–4 p.m.

The Oude Kerk (the Old Church, Oude Delft), which dates from 1250 with subsequent alterations. It has a magnificent pulpit and a number of monumental tombs, the most noteworthy being that of Piet Hein, who captured the Spanish Fleet in 1628.

Ascent of the tower
Apr.–Sept.: Mon.–Sat. 10 a.m.–noon, 1.30–4 p.m.

The Nieuwe Kerk (the New Church, Markt), a Gothic cruciform basilica with a high tower and the burial place of William of Orange. (Organ recitals in the summer.)

Times of opening
Tues.–Sat. 10 a.m.–5 p.m., Sun. and public holidays 1–5 p.m.; June–Aug.: Mon. 1–5 p.m.

Admission fee

The Prinsenhof: originally the Convent of St Agatha, after 1575 it served for a long time as the palace of the Princes of Orange. The Prinsenhof has a tragic place in Dutch history because it was here that William the Silent, the Prince of Orange to whom the country owed its independence, was assassinated in 1584. (Traces still remain at the foot of the steps!)

The picturesque buildings house the Stedelijk Museum (Oude Delft 185, entrance in St Agathaplein 1), devoted mainly to the 80-year war of Dutch Independence from Spain.

The oldest part of the convent has the only cloister (with double gallery) in the Netherlands.

The Prinsenhof is the venue for the annual antiques fair at the end of October as well as its famous concerts.

Times of opening
Tues.–Sat. 10 a.m.–5 p.m., Sun. and public holidays 1–5 p.m.; June–Aug.: 1–5 p.m.

The Stadhuis (town hall, Markt 87) has many 16th–18th c. paintings.

Museum Huis Lambert van Meerten (Oude Delft 199): an important collection of old furniture and paintings and a rich selection of Delftware.

Times of opening
mid–Apri.–Oct.: Tues.–Sat. 11 a.m.–5 p.m.

Museum Paul Tétar van Elven (Koornmarkt 67): furnished as an 18th c. mansion and true to its original style.

Delft: some of its famous tiles and an old street organ

Amsterdam Diamond Centre

Diamond-cutters at work

*Diamond cutting

Visits
See Practical Information, Diamonds

For many people Amsterdam is not only a jewel of a city but also a city of jewels, where diamond cutting and trading have been going on for centuries.

In the middle of the 16th c. many inhabitants of the area which is now Belgium fled to the Netherlands, to escape the Catholic Spaniards for religious reasons. Among the refugees who settled in Amsterdam were many diamond cutters. Thus there arose – to be exact in 1586 – the diamond industry, and in 1986 Amsterdam could celebrate its 400th anniversary as a diamond city. There followed periods of expansion and recession. In about 1750 the industry employed only about 600 people, but the discovery of diamonds in South America (in Brazil in particular) saw an unexpected upturn in its fortunes.

The world's first diamond exhibition was in Amsterdam in 1936.

During the Second World War tens of thousands of Jewish citizens of Amsterdam, including about 2000 diamond-cutters, were deported and never returned.

Today Amsterdam has at least a dozen firms of diamond-cutters and over 60 diamond-processors (see Practical Information, Diamonds).

Only about 20% of diamonds become gemstones (brilliants) for jewellery; the majority are used as industrial diamonds in drills, stone and glass cutters; in boring, grinding and polishing processes and in precision instruments, pick-ups, engraving tools, etc.

Today the trade mark of the diamond-cutters of Amsterdam is still a guarantee of outstanding workmanship and quality.

The largest diamond ever discovered, the famous Cullinan, known as the "Star of Africa", was processed in Amsterdam.

Driegrachtenhuis (House on three canals)

See Achterburgwal

*Edam

Location
15 km (9 miles) N (E10)

Buses
Stop opposite Centraal Station

VVV
See Practical Information, Information

The historic little town of Edam in North Holland is in the polder region on the IJsselmeer and is world-famous for its round red-skinned yellow cheeses.

Its people work in industry, agriculture, cattle-breeding and fisheries.

Edam grew up near the dam in the River E which linked the little River Purmer with the Zuider Zee. When, in 1230 the work was begun of damming the rivers flowing into the Zuider Zee (see General Information, Land reclamation, and Amsterdam A–Z: Zuider Zee), merchandise was transported here. Soon customs duties were levied and it became a trading post.

Edam obtained its charter in 1357 and enjoyed its heyday in the 16th–18th c. when shipbuilding, herring fishing and cheese brought economic prosperity to the town. (The warships in which Admiral de Ruyter defeated the English were built in Edam's shipyards.) In 1573 William of Orange granted Edam the right to its own weigh-house for its bravery and services in helping to lift the siege of Alkmaar.

Times of opening
Apr.–Sept.: 2–4.30 p.m.

The following buildings in Edam are worth a visit:

The Grote Kerk (or St Nicholas's Church Grote Kerkstraat).

Edam town hall

The late-Gothic church has a 15th c. tower and magnificent 17th c. stained-glass windows.

The Stadhuis (town hall) dating from 1737 on the Damplein. The registry office still has sand on the floor as it did in the Middle Ages. The council chamber, which is worth seeing in its own right, contains a small exhibition of paintings.

Times of opening
Mon.–Sat. 10 a.m.–4 p.m., Sun. 2–4 p.m.

The Stedelijk Museum, Damplein (municipal museum) in a house built in 1540 with an attractive façade dating from 1737 has a floating cellar built in the form of a ship.

Times of opening
Apr.–Sept.: 10 a.m.–5 p.m.

The Kaasmarkt (cheese weigh-house) where the original weights can still be seen.

The stretch of water between the two bridges on the Spuistraat is called "Boerenverdriet" ("farmers' dismay"), because the farmers' boats often used to get stuck here.

Boat trips

In July and August boat trips can be made on the Zuider Zee.

Flea market

See Vlooienmarkt

*Haven (Port) E–M 2–6

Buses
18, 21, 22, 28, 29, 32, 33, 34, 39, 46, 47 (central station)

Trams
1, 2, 4, 5, 9, 13, 16, 17, 24, 25 (central station)

Moorings
Steiger (de Ruijterkade)

The port of Amsterdam is 18·5 km (12 miles) from the open sea and, thanks to the IJmuiden sluices, is unaffected by the state of the tide. Several thousand ships call here annually, freighters and also passenger ships. There are regular services up the Rhine to Dusseldorf, Koblenz, Speyer, Strasburg and Basle. In addition Amsterdam is a popular starting point for cruises. Over 37,000 passengers use the port every year.

The port installations were begun in 1872 in conjunction with the construction of the North Sea Canal, the objective being to restore the former importance of the capital city which was being overtaken by Rotterdam. It is well worth joining one of the regular cruises around the harbour and canals, especially in the evening when the houses and bridges are illuminated.

The entire dock area was reclaimed from the IJ. Its channel was deepened and artificial islands with landing quays were built alongside. On the S bank of the IJ there is a series of large wet-docks including the Westerdok, the Oosterdok and the IJhaven, as well as important dockyards.

W of the Westerdok lie the Houthaven (timber), the Minervahaven, the Coenhaven and the spectacular Petroleumhaven, which gives access to the North Sea Canal.

Further W are the Westhaven with loading facilities for coal, crude oil, ore and grain, and with oil storage tanks, refineries and chemical plant.

On the N bank of the IJ there are several smaller docks and the locks of the North Holland Canal. Just W of the central station stands the 13-storey Port Administration building, built in 1958–60 by Dudok van Heel, which is 60 m (197 ft) high and has a restaurant with a panoramic view. The Scheepvaartmuseum (see Practical Information, Museum), the Dutch Maritime Museum, is located on the Oosterdok.

At the purpose-built Amsterdam Container Terminal container vehicles can be driven straight into the holds of the roll-on

Impressive both in the past and today: patrician houses on the Herengracht

roll-off vessels. The opening of the Amsterdam–Rhine Canal in 1952 made for considerably improved links with the European hinterland so far as bulk cargo handling is concerned.

Heineken Brewery H7

The Heineken brewery, one of the country's largest breweries, is on the corner of Stadhouderskade and Ferdinand Bolstraat, at least as long as it is still in Amsterdam. A move is planned. The brewery received its licence to brew beer in the mid-19th c. when it also bought up the old-established "Hooiberg" brewery which had been in existence since the Middle Ages.

Location
Stadhouderskade

Trams
5, 7, 10, 16, 24, 25

Visits
Mon.–Fri. 10–11.30 a.m. with beer-tasting (free)

Herengracht H5/6 (A1–4/B1, 4–5)

The origins of the Herengracht go back to the year 1612, when a plan to create a girdle of canals (Heren- Keizers- and Prinzengracht) was made. The project was completed in 1658. In Amsterdam's heyday (second half of 17th c.) the Herengracht was the most elegant residential district. To live here was so popular that the magistrate had to confine the width of the aristocrats' houses to 8 m, but of course there

Location
W and S of the centre

◀ *The port of Amsterdam: built on land reclaimed from the IJsselmeer*

were exceptions, such as the "House for a Prince" (No. 54). Behind the aristocratic houses with their magnificent façades (no fewer than 400 houses in the Herengracht are protected monuments), beautiful gardens were concealed, each of them exactly 51·5 m (169 ft) long. The layout of these gardens represented unbelievable luxury for a town which was on piles. A law declared that they could not be built on, an exception, however, was made for summer-houses and coach-houses. The "golden bocht", the golden arc of the Herengracht, with houses numbered 464–436 (between Vijzelstraat an Leidestraat) is especially noteworthy for its magnificently decorated houses. No. 527 Herengracht, built in 1667, has an interesting history; Tsar Peter the Great of Russia lived here during a visit to Holland. Today the patrician houses are mostly occupied by banks and offices or are used as museum buildings; they have become too large and too expensive to be used as dwellings. Here can be found the Theatrical Museum and the Willet Holthuysen Museum (see Practical Information; Museums) and also, at No. 470, the Goethe Institute.

The former Stadhuis (town hall, 1613; Nieuwstraat 23). Since the town hall moved to a new location, this building has been occupied by the Tourist Office.

The St Peterhof (1692), now an old people's home with a picturesque 17th and 18th c. interior.

Three 16th c. towers (inc. Oosterpoort).

Times of opening
Mon.–Fri. 11 a.m.–5 p.m., Sat., Sun. and public holidays 2–5 p.m.

A visit to the West Friesian Museum (Westfries Museum, Rodesteen 1), is highly recommended. It has collections of old paintings, porcelain, costumes and toys and in the cellar there is an archaeological department.

Old Dutch Market

An old Dutch market (Rodesteen) is held every Wednesday in July and August where ancient handicrafts are demonstrated by local people in period costume.

*Hoorn

Location
40 km (25 miles) N (A8, E10)

Buses
Stop opposite Centraal Station

VVV
See Practical Information, information

The town of Hoorn, in the Province of North Holland, the former capital of West Friesland on a bay in the IJsselmeer, is worth a visit. Its main claim to fame is that it used to be an international port, as its many historic buildings testify.
Today Hoorn is an important shopping, leisure, cultural and educational centre and is expected to become more important as a residential town because of its excellent communications with Alkmaar and Amsterdam.
In the 14th c. Hoorn quickly became the market centre of West Friesland and received its charter in 1356. In the second half of that century Hoorn already overshadowed the older towns of the Zuider Zee, Enkhuizen and Medemblik, and in the 16th c. the town became the major international port on the Zuider Zee. By the middle of the 17th c., however, Hoorn was already starting to decline in economic importance.
Hoorn numbers among its famous men Willem Schouten who sailed round the southern tip of America in 1616 and named it "Kap Hoorn" (Cape Horn) after his home town; Count Philip van Hoorn, a Knight of the Order of the Golden Fleece, who, together with Count Egmont, was executed in Brussels on

Hoorn town hall (Stadhuis), in a former monastery

5 June 1568 for his part in the Dutch Wars of Independence against Spain; and Jan Pieterszoon, Coen, Governor of the Dutch East Indies and founder of Batavia (now Djakarta, Indonesia).
Places worth visiting in Hoorn include:
The Noorderkerk, in Kleine Noord (North Church; built in 1426, restored in 1938), a hall basilica (with three naves of equal height), a late-Gothic spiral staircase and sumptuous Renaissance furnishings. The church is open to visitors during exhibitions.
The Oosterkerk, in Groote Oost (East Church; built 1450), a single-nave cruciform church with a Renaissance façade (1616). Its interior dates from the early 17th c. and the organ from 1765. For times of opening enquire at VVV.

Hortus Botanicus (Botanical garden of the Municipal University) D4

The botanical garden of the municipal university, with its exotic flowers, trees and plants, dates back to the time of the monastery herb gardens. The Vlooienburg botanical garden (with some 2000 native trees, plants, herbs and shrubs) came into existence in 1554 with the publication of a book about plants which described not only the plants themselves but also their healing properties. The garden was frequently relocated and enlarged and in 1877 became the property of the university. The Vrije University also maintains a botanical garden (see Practical Information, Parks). Admission fee.

Location
Plantage Middenlaan 2

Tram
9

Times of opening
Mon.–Fri. 9 a.m.–4 p.m.; Sat,. Sun. and public holidays
11 a.m.–4 p.m.

IJtunnel J5

Trams
1, 2, 4, 5, 9, 16, 24, 25

Over 100 years ago people were looking at ways of linking Amsterdam with the opposite bank of the IJ in the N (link with North Holland). A tunnel was being thought of even at that time (plans for a suspension bridge are even older), since the ferries to and from North Holland caused considerable delays. For a long time, however, such plans were thought unrealistic, and it was not until the beginning of this century that the city council was prepared seriously to examine the idea of a tunnel. From 1930 to 1950 countless designs were discussed and rejected but it was finally decided to build a tunnel for road vehicles only. Cyclists and pedestrians still have to use the ferries. On 25 May 1955 the first pile was driven into the ground but the project was dogged by organisational and financial problems and it was years before the work was completed at a total cost of over 20 million guilders. In October 1968 the tunnel was opened to traffic and brought great improvements in communications with North Holland.

Jodenbuurt (Jewish quarter) J6 (C/D 3/4)

Location
Around the Waterlooplein

Tram
9

The former Jewish quarter extends from the Houtkoopers-burgwal in the N to the Binnen-Amstel in the S. The first Jewish refugees came to Amsterdam at the end of the 16th c. and settled in the area around the Waterlooplein (Jodenbreestraat, Valkenburgerstraat, Oude Schans). They were mostly from Portugal (see Portuguese synagogue), but also from Germany and Poland. The Jewish quarter had a special charm, with its countless little second-hand shops, haberdashers and greengrocers.

A market used to be held on the Waterlooplein on Sundays, although it was hard to see how the dealers could make a living from selling their second-hand goods (see Vlooienmarkt). Of the former so charming Jewish quarter around the Waterloo-plein scarcely anything has survived the Second World War. With the deportation of the Jews during the war the quarter was robbed of its residents. In the 1960s the construction of an arterial road completely altered its appearance, and for the building of the Metro a cutting was made through the area. On Waterlooplein only one row of houses by the Amstel remained and these were pulled down in 1976; the last residents were expelled, the market (see Vlooienmarkt) closed and the area levelled. Nevertheless new life came back; today on Waterloo-plein stands Amsterdam's Opera House ("Het Muzeik-theater"), which together with the new Town Hall forms a double building.

Jordaan G 5–6/H5

Location
Between Prinsengracht and Lijnbaansgracht

To the W of the city centre, between Prinsengracht (see entry) and Lijnbaansgracht, lies the Jordaan, the working-class district made famous by the many songs about it. It came into being when the city was extended in the early 17th c. and many small craftsmen set up shop here. Refugees settled in the quarter during the Thirty Years War and artists (including Rembrandt) were so attracted by the Jordaan that they made their homes here.

Trams
3, 10, 13, 17

There are many theories about the name "Jordaan". The most likely is that it comes from the French word "jardin", meaning "garden", but whether or not the quarter owes its name to its many little front gardens and backyards there were certainly many Walloons and French living here when the Jordaan got its name.

Life in the Jordaan is still largely lived out on the streets. Originally this was for practical reasons (large families, small houses) but nowadays it is on grounds of sociability. The Jordaan still has its own special atmosphere, with convivial corner pubs, sweet-shops kept by little old ladies and tiny boutiques.

Many artists are irresistibly drawn to this quarter. The private foundation "Diogenes", which is concerned with providing places where artists and students can live, created, together with Claesz Claas Hofje, a residential complex for artists and students and, with the Jan Peiterz Huis, a place where musicians can practise.

* Kalverstraat H6 (A 3–4/B2–4)

Although Kalverstraat (between Dam and Munt, see entries) is no longer the meeting place for half Amsterdam, nevertheless in the meantime P. C. Hooftstraat is now considered the "fashionable address".

Trams
1, 2, 4, 5, 9, 16, 24, 25

First mentioned in 1393, it gets its name from the calf-trade. This does not necessarily mean that cattle-markets were actually held in this street, but we do know that cattle were driven through the Kalverstraat to the calf-market which took place on the Dam in the 16th c.

The first shopkeepers to settle in Kalverstraat were, of course, butchers, followed by craftsmen such as shoemakers and basketmakers. In the mid-18th c. there were over 200 shops of all kinds here, plus coffee-houses and boarding-houses.

Today Kalverstraat is a pedestrian precinct and attracts up to 100,000 shoppers a day. On Saturdays the crush is frightening. It can take half an hour to walk from the Munt to the Dam instead of the usual ten minutes – that is if you manage to get there at all and are not carried along by the crowd in quite a different direction.

Keizersgracht H5–6/J6 (A1, 2, 4/B4/C4)

The middle one of the three canals does not quite come up to the elegant standards of the Herengracht (see entry).

Location
W of Centraal Station to S of Rembrandtsplein

The finest houses are to be found between the Westermarkt and Vijzelstraat. This part was also famed in the last century for the "slipper parade" which took place here on Sundays after church when, between 2 and 4 in the afternoon, most of Amsterdam strolled up and down here in their Sunday best in order to see and be seen.

BOEKHANDEL VAN HET

Keukenhof: Holland's flower paradise

Famous houses on the Keizersgracht include:
The House with the Golden Chain (No. 268): an old mansion out of which hangs a golden chain. There are many legends purporting to explain the significance of this chain. According to one tale, a maid was accused of stealing a golden chain from her mistress but the chain was discovered in a crow's nest so the maid was reinstated.
Another story tells of a captain who lived in the house and had grown weary of going to sea. When forced to go to sea again for financial reasons, he swore to bring back a golden chain if fortune smiled on him or an iron chain if she did not. Obviously fortune smiled, hence the golden chain.
There are other traditional legends, but the true story seems to be that it was the home of a goldsmith and the golden chain, which has hung in front of the house since 1643, served as his trademark.
The House with the Heads (No. 123) dates from 1622 and is one of the finest mansions in the city. The gable is decorated with six helmeted heads, but there is also supposed to be a seventh female head. The story goes that it was the home of a rich merchant who had a deaf maid. One day when the maid was alone in the house thieves broke in but were all beheaded by the maid.
Today it houses offices.

*Keukenhof

Location
Lisse, 35 km (20 miles) SW

The Keukenhof, in the heart of the Dutch flower-growing area between Haarlem and Leiden (see entry), has since 1949 been

◀ *Keizersgracht: a reminder of Amsterdam's venerable past*

Rail
From Centraal Station to Haarlem and Leiden

Times of opening
end of Mar. to end of May: daily 8 a.m.–6.30 p.m.
Admission fee

a special place for an excursion: the National Flower Exhibition takes place here every year from the end of March to the end of May on a 28 hectare (69 acre) site.
Apart from every imaginable type of bulb the Keukenhof also has shrubs such as rhododendrons and azaleas. Even before the flowers in the grounds are in bloom, hundreds of thousands of crocuses, hyacinths, narcissi and, above all, tulips can be admired in huge greenhouses (5000 sq. m/53,820 sq. feet) from 9 in the morning until sunset. In the Juliana Pavilion and the Konigin Beatrix Pavilion exhibitions and other events are held.
From the second half of April until the beginning of May the five million flowers in the grounds of the Keukenhof are at the height of their splendour and there is a magnificent view of it all from a windmill.

** Koninklijk Paleis (Royal palace) A2

Trams
1, 2, 4, 5, 9, 13, 16, 17, 24, 25

Open during the summer Mon.–Sat. 12.30–4 p.m.; at other times guided tours on Wed. at 2 p.m.

Admission free

The Royal Palace on the Dam (see entry), formerly the town hall, constitutes an impressive central point of Amsterdam. Nowadays it serves as the Queen's residence when she is in the city.
Building began on 20 January 1648 with the sinking of the first of 13,659 piles for the new town hall. Its architect was Jacob van Campen whose inspiration was the architecture of Ancient Rome; the exterior is strictly classical and the interior is magnificently furnished. The apartments are decorated with a wealth of reliefs, ornamentation and marble sculpture by the Flemish sculptors Artus Quellinus and Rombout Verhulst, and with friezes and ceiling-paintings by Ferdinand Bol and Govert Flinck, pupils of Rembrandt.
Van Campen was, however, unable to finish the building and Stalpaert took over from him in 1654. Costs had risen so much in the meantime that work on the tower of the New Church (see Nieuwe Kerk) had to be suspended. The new town hall with the 51 m (167 ft) high tower (carillon) was finally completed in 1665. For about 200 years this imposing building, the greatest work of the 17th c. Dutch Classicism, was the political centre of Amsterdam and the republic. In 1808, however, Louis Napoleon, Holland's new king, wanted it for his own residence. His Empire furniture from that time is still one of the finest collections in the world. With the ending of Napoleonic rule the town hall reverted to the city which, however, because of its financial straits, was unable to use it for its original purpose and let it to King William I as a temporary residence. In 1935 the State bought the palace for 10 million guilders and had it extensively restored for use on official occasions.
The finest rooms, and the most interesting from the art historian's point of view, are those overlooking the Dam. The city treasurer's room has an interesting marble fireplace and ceiling paintings by Cornelius Holsteyn. The Hall of the Aldermen contains paintings by Ferdinand Bol and Govert Flinck and a work by Jan Lievens hangs in the Mayor's Chamber.
The largest and most important room is the Council Hall (34×16·75 m (112×55 ft) and 28 m (92 ft) high). This

The impressive Koninklijk Paleis on the Dam ▶

sumptuously decorated hall (one of the most beautiful state rooms in Europe) was where the ball celebrating the marriage of the Crown Princess Beatrix to Claus von Amsberg was held in 1966.
Mention should also be made of the ante-room (Vierschaar) which contains four outstanding caryatids (figures supporting beams) by A. Quellinus the Elder.

*Leiden

Location
40 km (25 miles) SW

Rail
From Centraal Station via Schiphol, on completion of the rail link to the airport

VVV
See Practical Information, Information

The old university town of Leiden (or Leyden) in the Province of South Holland lies on the sluggish Old Rhine which flows like a canal through the town. For many centuries it was an industrial town, and was known in the Middle Ages for its cloth-weaving. Nowadays its major industries are machinery and printing (its far-eastern prints are world-famous). Leiden has several historic buildings, a great many museums and the largest indoor cattle market in the Netherlands.
In the 12th c. the Counts of Holland built first a castle then a palace (where Floris V was born) on a rise overlooking the Old Rhine. The little town of Leiden grew up between the castle and the palace and received its charter in 1266. In the 14th c. the town was the centre of the cloth industry. On 3 October 1574 William of Orange freed Leiden from the Spanish siege which, accompanied by plague and starvation, had lasted almost a year, and this event is still annually celebrated.
In 1575 the town was rewarded for its bravery with a university which later became an important European centre of culture.

The university building: the chapel of a former monastery

Several important artists and scholars were born here in the 17th c. including Rembrandt van Rijn (1606–69), Jan Steen (1626–79), Gerard Dou (1613–75) and Herman Boerhave (1668–1738).

The following are worth visiting:
The imposing castle at Burgsteeg 14 (restored 1970) on a hill overlooking the confluence of the Old and the New Rhine, from which there is a fine panoramic view.

Times of opening
Mon.–Sat. 8 a.m.–11 p.m., Sun. 11 a.m.–11 p.m.

The University on the Rapenburg. The former chapel of a Dominican monastery has served as the old university building since 1581.

The 17th c. Stadhuis (town hall) with carillon in Breestraad. Its splendid Renaissance façade was almost completely destroyed by fire in 1929 but it has been partially restored in the old style.

Times of opening
by arrangement (tel. 0711 25 49 11)

St Pieterskerk in Pieterskeerkhof (built *c.* 1315), a late-Gothic cruciform basilica (the tower collapsed in 1512 and was never rebuilt) with an impressive pulpit and various tombs, including that of John Robinson, the leader of the Pilgrim Fathers, who in 1611 founded in Leiden the first community of Independents (Puritans driven out of England).

Times of opening
Mon.–Sat. 1.30–4 p.m.

The Gravensteen, with its Classical façade, originally a prison, first for the counts and then for the town, is now attached to the University Law Faculty. It is not open to the public.

The museums include:

The Stedelijk Museum (Municipal Museum), Oude Singel 28–32, in the Lakenhal (Cloth Hall, 1639), formerly the headquarters of the cloth-weavers guild. It houses important 17th–18th c. paintings (including Corm, Lucas van Leyden, Rembrandt, Jan Steen) and an exhibition on old weaving techniques (Oude Singel 28–30).

Times of opening
Tues.–Sat. 10 a.m.–5 p.m., Sun. and public holidays 1–5 p.m. Oct: 10 a.m.–noon

The National Archaeological Museum (Rijksmuseum van Oudheden, Rapenburg 28) with a large collection of Greek, Etruscan and Roman sculpture, ancient vases and artefacts, as well as archaeological finds primarily from the Netherlands.

Times of opening
2 Jan.–2 Oct.: Tues.–Sat. 10 a.m.–5 p.m., Sun. and public holidays 1–5 p.m.

The Botanical Garden (Hortus Botanicus), Rapenburg 73, dating from 1587, is also worth visiting.

Times of opening
May–Sept.: Mon.–Fri. 8.30 a.m.–5.30 p.m., Sun. and public holidays 2–5 p.m. (gardens)

Leidseplein G6

Trams
1, 2, 6, 7, 10

Amsterdam's second-largest amusement and entertainment centre (after the Rembrandtplein) caters for all tastes with two theatres (the Municipal Theatre and De Balie, formerly a prison), countless cinemas, hotels and restaurants in every price-category, night clubs, bars, cabarets and pubs. From Shakespeare to striptease, it's all there on the Leidseplein which pulsates with life until well into the night.
The lively atmosphere of the Leidseplein is not a modern phenomenon. It was here that the farmers used to leave their carts and have their horses looked after when they came into town for the market. Today the square's cosmopolitan

atmosphere comes from the Stadschouwburg (Municipal Theatre – see entry), the Hotel Américain and pavement cafés (including the Café Reynders, a meeting-place for artists and journalists) and, last but not least, the many visitors both from home and abroad.

Lieverdje A3

Location
Spui

Trams
1, 2

The Lieverdje on the Spui (an Amsterdam street-urchin) was originally a plaster figure made by the sculptor Carel Kneulman for a local festival. A manufacturer found the lad so appealing that he had it cast in bronze and presented it to the city.

It was unveiled on the Spui on 10 September 1960 and has since proved a favourite rallying point for political action because of its central position near the university, and as an anti-Establishment symbol.

In the mid-sixties it was here that the "Provos", the spontaneous young people's movement of that time, mounted 'happenings' and handed out their first manifestos.

Magere Brug (Mager bridge) C4

Tram
4

Metro

Of Amsterdam's 1000 or so bridges the "Magere Brug" near the Weesperstraat is the most photographed.

This simple wooden drawbridge over the Amstel was built in 1671 as a footbridge. After being renovated several times it was

Magere Brug: the most photographed of all Amsterdam's bridges

Marken: dancing on the ice

demolished in 1929. It was to be replaced by a modern electrically operated bridge but it was finally decided to build a wooden reconstruction of the original.
The building work was supervised by the architect Mager who gave his name to the bridge.

Marken

Location
22 km (14 miles) NE

Rail
From Centraal Station

Bus
From opposite Centraal Station

VVV
See Practical Information, Information: Monnickendam

Marken used to be an island in the IJsselmeer but since 1957 it has been linked to the Nes headland by a 2 km (1¼ miles) long dyke. This dyke is one of the ring of dykes that will encircle the Markerwaard polder which is to be the fourth area reclaimed from the Zuider Zee (see Zuider Zee and General Information, Land Reclamation).
Since fishing lost its importance with the damming of the Zuider Zee, tourism has become the main source of income for the peninsula and 80% of Marken's population work outside the area.
In 1232 Marken was a monastic settlement attached to the Friesian abbey of Mariengaard which owned the whole island from 1251 to 1345 when it was bought by the city of Amsterdam. This meant that in the Middle Ages it was often the scene of the quarrels that determined the relationship between Amsterdam and the ports on the opposite bank of the Zuider Zee (e.g. Kampen). In the 17th c. shipping flourished here, and Marken became independent during the French occupation (*c.* 1811). By the late 19th c. Marken had 17 residential

districts, but today there are only seven villages in addition to the main village of Kerkbuurt.

The principal attraction for tourists in Marken are the architecture of its houses – until 1931 the wooden houses were built on piles – and the folk costumes which are still worn there. The women wear a "ryglyf", a type of semi-transparent bodice that is either dark blue or embroidered with various colours.

The island is still very Calvinist, so one should not expect to be invited to a winter wedding which is best celebrated on the frozen Zuider Zee – in the traditional costumes, of course, with music and folk dancing, the women dancing together.

The people of Marken still hold an Easter procession.

Times of opening
Easter–Oct.: Mon.–Sat. 10 a.m.–4.30 p.m., Sun. noon–4 p.m.

In the local museum of Marken (Marker Museum, Kerbuurt 44–47) the visitor can see a vivid representation of everyday life of the inhabitants of the former island.

Monnickendam

Location
13 km (8 miles) NE

Buses
Stop opposite Centraal Station

Motorboat
From Stationsplein or de Ruijterkade (summer only)

VVV
See Practical Information, Information

Monnickendam is a small old town in North Holland on the banks of the Gouwzee and the IJsselmeer and its location explains why it is best known for its smoked fish and as a centre for water sports.

About 70% of Monnickendam's working population have jobs elsewhere and the rest are in business and tourism.

Monnickendam was founded by monks in the 12th c. and was granted its charter in 1335. Its position on the Zuider Zee (see entry) with its busy shipping trade soon brought it fame and prosperity but by the 17th c. only fishing remained as an important source of income, and life in Monnickendam had adjusted accordingly. Various catastrophes also struck the town: in 1297 it was raided by the Friesians and in 1494 and 1514 large sections of the town were destroyed by fire.

Some of the places of interest:

Times of opening
Mid-June to mid-Aug.: 10.30 a.m.–12.30 p.m., 2–4 p.m., Sun. 2–4.30 p.m.

The Belfry (Speeltoren, in Noordeinde) dating from the 16th c. with its 18-bell carillon (1596). It is not open to the public.

The Groote Kerk (or St Nicholas's Church, in Zarken, built in 1400) which houses a collection of tiles and majolica ware.

Times of opening
By appointment: tel. 02995/3939

The Stadhuis (town hall), at Noordeinde 5, originally built as a private mansion in 1746, has a council chamber with golden wallpaper and a Rococo ceiling.

Be sure to visit the "Haringhallen" eel-smoking establishments (Palingrokerejen).

From Monnickendam boat trips can be made to Marken and Volendam between April and September daily from 9 a.m. –4.45 p.m.

*Mozes-en-Aaronkerk (Moses and Aaron Church) C3

Location
Jodenbreestraat

Underground station
Waterlooplein

The history of this church goes back to the "Alteratie" (see General Information, History of the City) when secret churches sprang up everywhere, since Catholics no longer dared to hold services in public. In 1641 Father Boelenzs purchased the Moses and Aaron House in Jodenbreestraat from a rich Jew

Mozes-en-Aaronkerk: once a "secret" Catholic church, now a youth centre ►

Tram
9

and converted it into a church. In the course of time the church was enlarged, and it was consecrated in 1841, after its transformation into its present neo-Classical form by a Belgian architect.
Today the Moses and Aaron Church is no longer a house of God but a youth club where yoga is taught, tea dispensed and sitar concerts given. There are still times, however, when foreign workers threatened with deportation come here in search of a secret refuge.

Muntplein with Munttoren (Mint tower) B4

Trams
4, 9, 16, 24, 25

The main shopping streets, Rokin, Kalverstraat (see entry) and Reguliersbreestraat, start from the Muntplein.
In the 15th c. this square on the Amstel next to the city wall, known at the time as Sheep Square, was where the sheep market was held. Its present name dates from 1672 when money was coined in the Mint (the former guardroom next to the Mint tower).

Munttoren (Mint tower)

The name "Mint tower" dates from 1672 when, for two years, Amsterdam was the site of the mint while the French occupied Utrecht where coins were usually minted. The Munttoren is part of the medieval city walls which were almost completely destroyed in the great fire of 1818. The lower part of the tower was left standing. On the remaining stones the city architect Henrick de Keyser placed a wooden structure (with a carillon by Hemony) and a gilded weather-vane in the shape of an ox, as a reminder of the calf-market which had been held on the nearby Dam (see entry). When this weather-vane fell from the top of the tower during a storm in 1840 it was replaced by the usual weather-cock.

Museum Amstelkring C2

Location
Oudezijds Voorburgwal 40

Trams
4, 9, 16, 24, 25

Metro

Times of opening
Mon.–Sat. 10 a.m.–5 p.m.;
Sun. and public holidays
1–5 p.m.

Closed
1 Jan.

Admission fee

The museum, with a "secret" Catholic church, is nicknamed "Ons' Lieve Heer op Zolder" ("Our dear Lord in the Attic"). After the Reformation, when the Catholics had to hold their services in secret, a secret oratory for around 200 believers was set up under the roof of this private house. If danger threatened there was a way out through the skylight.
After the death of its Catholic owner the house fell into the hands of non-Catholics, but services still took place here until 1888.
Later the Amstelkring foundation turned the house and church into a museum in which the atmosphere of the 17th c. "secret church" can still be experienced today. Besides the original oratory (with organ and altar), private 18th c. chambers housing a collection of church antiquities, pictures and engravings are also open to visitors.
The museum still functions as a church. Concerts of Baroque music are also held here in the winter months.

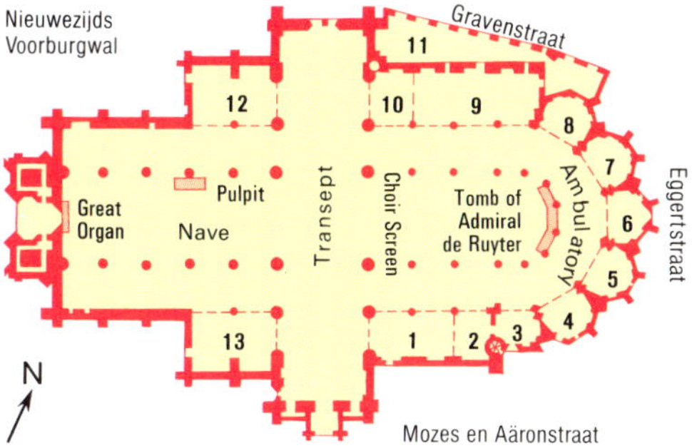

Nieuwe Kerk
St Catherine

1 Sanctuary
2 Eggert Chapel
3 Chapel of Our Lady of the Seven Sorrows (Sills Chapel)
4 Chapel of concealment
5 Meeus Chapel
6 Bricklayers' Chapel
7 Boelens Chapel
8 Cloth-workers' Chapel
9 Crucifix Chapel
10 Chapel of Our Lady
11 Deaconry
12 Old Crucifix Choir
13 Headmaster's house

* Nieuwe Kerk (New Church) A/B2

Location
Dam

Trams
1, 2, 4, 5, 9, 13, 16, 17, 24, 25

Times of opening
Mon.–Sat. 11 a.m.–4 p.m., Sun. noon–5 p.m.

Closed
Jan. and Feb.

The Coronation church of the Dutch monarchs (since 1814) lies in the heart of the city next to the Royal Palace (see Koninklijk Paleis) on the Dam (see entry), and its most recent great event (after 22 years of renovation work) was the coronation of Queen Beatrix on 30 April 1980.

The church is no longer used for services. Antique fairs, art exhibitions and regular organ concerts take place here.

Strangely enough this church has only a small tower instead of a high steeple. The money for something larger was not forthcoming because it had been used to build the Royal Palace.

The church dates from the early 15th c. Its foundation charter is dated 1408 when the Bishop of Utrecht granted the city of Amsterdam the right to have a second parish (the first was that of the Oude Kerk – see entry).

The Amsterdam banker William Eggert presented the site. After his death he was buried in the church and his son had a chapel named after him built on to the church.

When Amsterdam was ravaged by fire in 1421 and 1452 the New Church suffered considerable damage, but in each case was quickly restored. Its present aspect dates roughly from 1490.

The imposing late-Gothic cruciform basilica was almost completely burnt down in 1645 owing, it is said, to the carelessness of a craftsman. After its reconstruction, which took about three years, the church was reconsecrated with a service of thanksgiving for the Peace of Münster (1648).

The magnificent pulpit (1649) by Albert Vinckenbrink, a marvel of Baroque woodcarving, is decorated with the four evangelists and figures symbolising Faith, Hope, Charity, Justice and Prudence. The church has a notable organ of 1670, the case of which was designed by Jacob van Campen, an exceptionally beautiful choir screen, cast in bronze, and fine choir-stalls.

Of great interest are the tombs of many famous Dutchmen, including P. C. Hooft and Nicholas Tulp and the Baroque tomb of Admiral Michiel de Ruyter (d. 1679) by the high altar.

The stained-glass windows are also interesting: one of them (dated 1650) depicts the granting of the city's coat of arms by Willam IV; the Queen's Window (1898) commemorates the coronation of Queen Wilhelmina.

Nieuwmarkt C2/3

Location
Nieuwmarkt

Metro
Nieuwmarkt

Buses
22, 25

There actually used to be a market on the Nieuwmarkt in the 17th and 18th c. and it was divided up into individual plots for the stalls selling cheese, fish, herbs and cloth.
During the Second World War the Nieuwmarkt was widely known for its flourishing Black Market.
In 1975 there were street riots in this area when the local people gave vent to their anger at the demolition of many houses for the construction of the Underground.
The Nieuwmarkt is the site of the Waaggebouw (see entry), built as a gateway to the city in 1488, which houses the Museum of the history of Amsterdam's Jewish population and the Museum of Medicine and Pharmacy.

Olympisch Stadion (Olympic Stadium) E/F8

Location
Stadionplein

Buses
CN 1, 9, 11, 19

Trams
16, 24

Amsterdam's most important sports centre is the Olympic Stadium. Built in 1928 when the Olympic Games were held in the Netherlands, it originally held 40,000 spectators but after being extended in 1936 it now holds 60,000. Athletic and speedway meetings and cycle races take place in the stadium.

*Oude Kerk (Old Church) B/C2

Location
Ouderkerksplein

Trams
4, 9, 16, 24, 25

Metro

Amsterdam's oldest church was built in 1306 as a small cruciform church to replace a wooden church which is thought to have been built here in about 1300. It was the first hall church (i.e. with the aisles the same height as the nave) in North Holland and the model for other churches in the region (e.g. in Edam). It was dedicated to St Nicolaas by the Bishop of Utrecht.

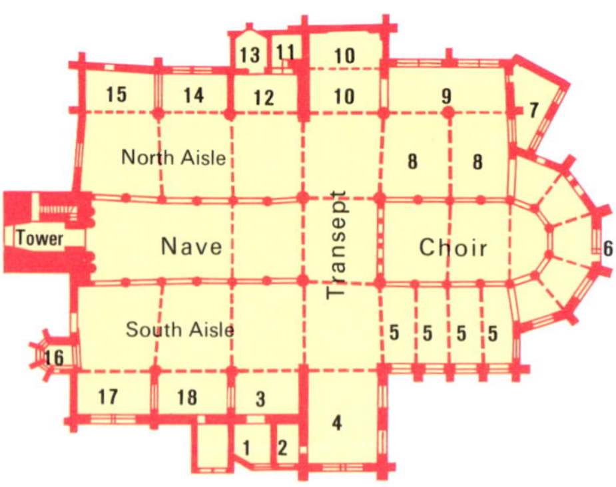

Oude Kerk
St Nicolaas

1 South Portal (entrance)
2 Iron Chapel
3 Smiths' Chapel
4 St Sebastian's Chapel
5 Seamen's Chapel
6 Remains of the former Chapel of the Holy Tomb
7 Chamber of the Guild of Our Lady
8 Old Female Choir
9 New Female Choir (stained glass)
10 Tomb of St Joris
11 Holy Tomb
12 Buckwheat Merchants' Chapel
13 Old North Portal (c. 1520)
14 Shippers' Chapel
15 Hamburg Chapel
16 Former Baptistery (c. 1462)
17 Lijsbeth Gaven Chapel
18 Chapel of the Poor

Oude Kerk: Amsterdam's oldest church ▶

Times of opening
Church: Mon.–Sat.
10 a.m.–4 p.m.
Tower: 1 June–15 Sept.
Mon., Thurs. 2–5 p.m.
Tues., Wed. 11 a.m.–2 p.m.

There were soon plans for enlarging it and in 1370 two chapels were built on to the choir and an ambulatory added. The church was spared the two great fires which devastated Amsterdam in the Middle Ages. Other chapels were partly endowed by guilds. The large side chapels were added around 1500. The alterations to the choir in the 16th c. were financed (as was usual in those days) by a lottery. Also dating from this period is a portal on the S side which gives access to the "iron" chapel, where the documents showing the city's privileges, including the freedom from tolls granted in 1275, were kept behind an iron door, until they were finally transferred to the municipal archives in 1872.
The tower was also remodelled in the 16th c. and the low Gothic tower was replaced by the present high W tower. This has a carillon (by Hemony, 1658) which is among the finest in the country. It is possible to climb to the top of the tower which affords a fine view over Amsterdam.
The interior of the church, now Protestant, has features dating from before the Reformation, including three magnificent windows (1555) from the Dutch High Renaissance, and finely carved wooden choir-stalls.
Many famous citizens of Amsterdam are buried here, including Rembrandt's wife Saskia and deserving admirals.

Oudemanhuispoort B3

Location
Between Grimburgwal and Kloveniersburgwal

Trams
4, 5, 9, 16, 24, 25

Times of opening
Mon.–Sat. 10 a,m,–4 p.m.

This arcade has a number of antiquarian bookshops and bookstalls with "oude mannetjes" (little old men) behind the counter. As its name "old men's gateway" indicates, the arcade used to be the entrance to an old people's home. Above the entrance there are still allusions to old age: a pair of spectacles and two old men.

Oudewater

Location
42 km (26 miles) S

VVV
See Practical Information, Information

Times of opening
Mid-April–mid-Sept.:
Tues.–Sat. 10 a.m.–5 p.m.,
Sun. and public holidays
noon–5 p.m.

Oudewater, in the Province of Utrecht, is chiefly known for its "witch scales" (Heksenwaag) from 1595, on which alleged witches were weighed until 1754 and usually found to be too heavy. Even in those days very few Dutchwomen would have weighed less than 50 kg (8 st) on the scales, and if one weighed more she could not be a witch because otherwise her broomstick would have collapsed under her weight. This "witches' friend" can still be seen today (Leeuweringerstraat 2).
The historical little town with its narrow canals makes a living today from agriculture, industry and services, although roughly 60% of the working population have jobs elsewhere.
Oudewater was inhabited as early as the end of the 10th c. and belonged to the bishopric of Utrecht. It received its charter in 1265 but was pledged to Floris V of Holland in 1280. This pledge was in fact never redeemed, so that Oudewater remained part of the Province of South Holland until 1970. The town served Floris V as a frontier fortress which involved it in many disputes, insurrections and sieges, even in later years.
There was peace, however, in the religious field, so that Oudewater became a haven for many Catholic refugees. Trade and industry flourished here in the late Middle Ages.

Besides its many old houses with stepped gables, visitors should also see the 14th c. church (Norderheerkstraat 20), whose tower has a saddleback roof and carillon (*c.* 1300), the town hall (Stadhuis, Visbrug 1) with its Renaissance façade (restored in 1973).

Portugese Synagoge (Portuguese synagogue) D3/4

Location
J. D. Meijerplein

Bus
56

Tram
9

Metro

The Portuguese synagogue, the largest of the three houses of worship on the J. D. Meijerplein, is reached through a forecourt surrounded by small houses (including the sexton's house, the Tes Haim library and the Livraria Montezinos).The building, completed in 1675 and facing SE towards Jerusalem, was modelled on the temple of Solomon. The finest building of the Jewish faith in the Netherlands, it contains an ark of the covenant made of rare Brazilian wood and splendid menorahs. The synagogue was restored between 1953 and 1959.

Prinsengracht G5–6/H5–7

Location
Between Prinsenstraat and Amstelveld

Trams
13, 17

The Prinsengracht is less elegant than either the Keizersgracht or the Herengracht (see entries) and therefore livelier and busier. The rents of the houses here are much more reasonable; there are relatively fewer banks and offices but many snug little cafés.

Prinsengracht: gracious living behind old façades

Rembrandthuis

Rembrandt: modelled in wax

*Rembrandthuis (Rembrandt's house) C3

Location
Jodenbreestraat 4–6

Tram
9

Metro

Times of opening
Mon.–Sat. 10 a.m.–5 p.m., Sun. and public holidays 1–5 p.m.

Closed 1 Jan

Rembrandt, with his wife Saskia, spent his happiest and most successful years when pupils and commissions poured in, in this house on the Jodenbreestraat which is now the Rembrandt museum. It was in this quarter, where Jews had settled (see Jodenbuurt) from all over the world, that he found the models for his Biblical themes. Here he painted what he had seen during the day on his outings along the canals and the Amstel. The house in which Rembrandt lived for about 20 years has again been furnished in the style of the 17th c. and contains numerous etchings and drawings as well as the painter's own personal objects. Admission fee.

Rembrandtsplein (Rembrandt Square) B4

Trams
4, 9

Besides the Leidseplein (see entry) the Rembrandtsplein is the most important leisure centre in the city, albeit different in character. There are cafés and eating places here, too, but the Rembrandtsplein is predominantly the quarter for night clubs and striptease establishments.
The square, in which the buttermarket used to be held, has always been a centre of social life. When fairs were held here it swarmed with people in search of the abundance of

entertainments to be found in the booths and at the many stalls. When the buttermarket was discontinued in the mid-19th c. the square retained its atmosphere as somewhere to stroll and find amusement. It was then that it acquired its present name when the little park was laid out with its statue of Rembrandt.

**Rijksmuseum (National Museum) G/H7

The world-famous museum of art goes back to the time of King Louis Napoleon who wanted to make Amsterdam a centre for art and science. In 1809 he set up the Grand Musée Royal in his palace (see Koninklijk Paleis) on the Dam (see entry). Works from the national museum in The Hague, which had been opened in 1798, and a few pieces belonging to the city (including Rembrandt's "Night Watch") formed the basis for this museum, which grew swiftly with the purchase of various collections.

Soon the palace rooms could no longer hold all the works, so eight years after its foundation the National Museum was transferred to the Trippenhuis (see entry). More purchases and gifts over the next few years made another move inevitable. It was finally decided that a museum in neo-Gothic should be built on the Stadhouderskade (1877–85). The architect was Pieter Henryk Johannes Cuypers.

Today the Rijksmuseum has about 7 million works of art, including 5000 paintings in over 250 rooms, a library with some 35,000 volumes and about 21,000 auction catalogues. Apart from its unique collection of old masters, it offers an

Entrances
Stadhouderskade 42
Jan Luykenstraat la
Hobbemastraat 19

Telephone
732 121

Trams
1, 2, 5, 16, 24, 25

Times of opening
Tues.–Sat. 10 a.m.–5 p.m.;
Sun. and public holidays
1–5 p.m.

Closed
1 Jan. and Mon.

Admission fee

Guided tours
English and French

The most famous painting in the Rijksmuseum: Rembrandt's "Night Watch"

Rijksmuseum

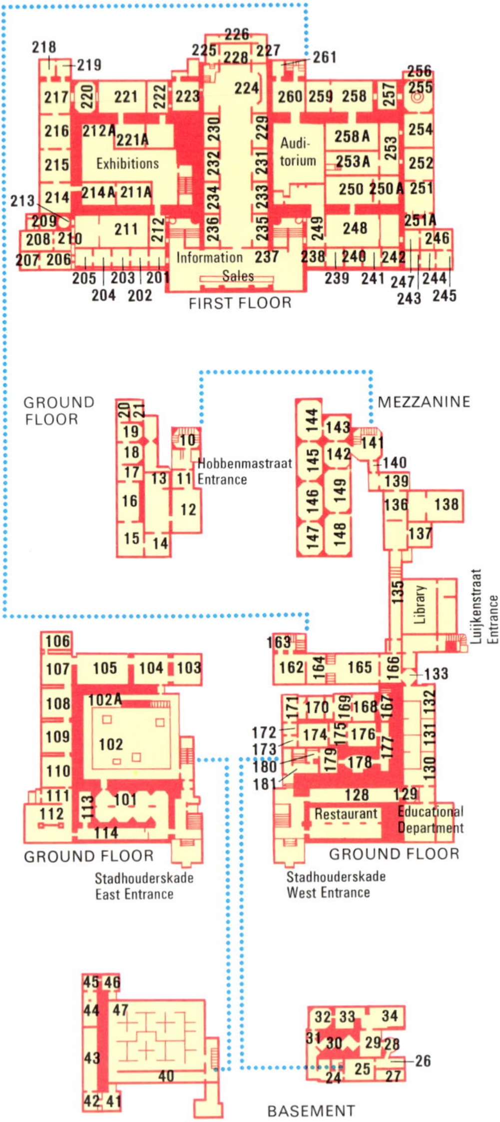

FIRST FLOOR – paintings

- 201–202 Dutch painters of the 15th c.: Geertgen to Sint Jans, Jan Mostaert
- 203–209 Dutch painters of the 16th c.
- 204 Lucas van Leyden
- 205 Jan van Scorel, Maerten van Heemskerck
- 206 Pieter Aertsz, Joachim Bueckelaer
- 209 Joose de Momper
- 210–228 Dutch painters of the 17th c.
- 210 Werner van den Valckert
- 211 Thomas de Keyser, Pieter Saenredam
- 211/211A Frans Hals (portraits)
- 212 Sale of reproductions and catalogues
- 214A Jan van Goyen, Hendrik Averkamp, Esaias van de Velde
- 214 Jacob van Ruisdael, Adriaen van Ostade
- 215 Bartholomeus van der Helst, Paulus Potter, Jan van de Cappelle, Adriaen van de Velde, Aert van de Neer
- 216 Jan Steen, Aelbert Cuyp
- 217–219 Dutch paintings with Italian motifs: Asselijn, Berchem, Both, Dujardin; Willem van de Velde the Younger: "View of the Ij off Amsterdam"
- 220–224 Rembrandt van Rijn: portraits, biblical and historical scenes
- 220 First Rembrandt Hall, inc. "Jeremiah Lamenting the Destruction of Jerusalem"
- 221A Paintings from Rembrandt's later years, inc. "Staalmeesters"
- 222/222A Rembrandt's pupils, inc. Govert Flinck, Ferdinand Bol, Nicolaes Maes
- 224 The "Night Watch" (original title: "The company of Captain Frans Banning Cocq and Lieutenant Willem van Ruytenburgh". It shows the moment when the Captain is giving his Lieutenant order for the guards' deployment)
- 225–228 Johannes Vermeer, Pieter de Hooch, Gerard ter Borch, Gerard Dou
- 226 Vermeer van Delft: "The Love Letter", "Young Woman Reading a Letter", Pieter de Hooch
- 227 Gerard ter Borch
- 229–232 Italian painters: Fra Angelico
- 236 Tiepolo, etc.
- 233 Spanish painters, inc. Goya and Murillo
- 234 French painters
- 235 Rubens, Van Dyck, etc.

MEZZANINE – paintings

135–149 Dutch paintings from 1700 to 1900; non-European art
135 Willem and Frans van Mieris, Adriaen and Pieter van de Werff
136–137 Cornelis Troost, Jacob de Wit
138 Islamic art: carpets, ceramics, etc.
139 Pastels by J. E. Liotard and C. Troost
141 Staircase: Chinese porcelain
142–149 Paintings from the late 18th to 19th c.
142 Jan Ekel the Younger, Adriaan de Lelie
143 Pieter Kleyn, Wouter van Troostwijk; Jelgerhuis, Van Os, Wybrand Hendriks
144–145 Nuyen, J. A. Kruseman, B. C. Koekkoek
146 Hague School: watercolours
147–148 Hague School: Willem, Jacob and Matthijs Maris, Anton Mauve, Jozef Israels, etc.
149 Amsterdam Impressionism: G. H. Breitner

FIRST FLOOR – Sculpture and decorative art

238–251 Dutch artists from the Middle Ages until the early 20th c.
238 Limoges enamels
239 Bronze statues from a tomb
241–242 15th and 16th c. sculpture inc. the "Death of the Virgin" and "Angel Musicians" by Adriaen van Wezel
242 Tapestry c. 1500, the "Orange Harvest"
243 Gothic furniture
246 Altar from Antwerp with scenes of the Passion
247 Ecclesiastical robes and silver
248 Tapestry (Brussels c. 1510) and a Gothic rood screen from a church in North Brabant; art of the Italian Renaissance: bronze sculpture, majolica, furniture
250/250A Tapestries from Delft (F. Spiering)
251 17th c. furniture, majolica
251A "Treasure Chamber": jewels, corporation silver (16th c.)
252 Room with fine panelling
253 Valuable Flemish Baroque items; glass and silverware
253A Art of the former Dutch colonies (showing the way of life)
254 Silver room: silversmiths' art (Vianen, Lutma)
255–257 Delftware collection
258 Terracotta by Artus Quellinus; sculpture
258A Tapestries with hunting scenes (c. 1650)
259 Furniture, gilded leather hangings, ivory carving
260 Furniture made of rare woods
261 Chinese screens

GROUND FLOOR – Dutch history

101 Clocks, watches and other 15th/16th c. items; documents from the uprising against the Spanish, including portraits of statesmen and military commanders (William of Orange)
102 Courtyard "Square of the 17th c."; ships, arms, armour and a colonial history collection
102A Everyday life in the 17th c.
103 Room of sea warfare: ships, captured flags, paintings by Van de Velde, the Elder and the Younger
104 Admirals' room: portraits and arms
105 The French invasion of 1672 and the time of the Stadhouder William III
106 Colonial history, especially the Dutch presence in Ceylon, Japan and China
107–108 History of the Netherlands in the 18th c.
109 The Annexation of the Netherlands into the French Empire; huge painting by Pieneman commemorating the Battle of Waterloo
110 United Kingdom room, Belgium
111–112 Dutch history of the 19th and 20th c.
113 Exhibition on the Second World War
114 Recorded information

Print room

128–133 Temporary exhibitions of drawings and prints

Sculpture and decorative art

162 Dolls' houses
163 Dutch sculpture
164–165 Arts and crafts from the time of Stadhouder William III
166 Lace
167 Tapestries
168–169 Dutch and French 18th c. furniture
170–171 Collection of Dresden china
172 Japanese Kakiemon porcelain
173 Small articles of French Louis XV furniture
174 Dutch furniture from c. 1750; two large paintings by Jacob de Wit
175 Delftware and foreign ceramics
176 French furniture, including the desk of the Elector of Trier by Abraham and David Roentgen
177 18th c. Dutch silverware
178 French furniture transition phase from Rococo to Louis XVI
179 Room with Louis XVI furniture and Sèvres porcelain
180 Trinkets: 18th c. snuff boxes, clocks and jewellery
181 18th c. ecclesiastical art

Asiatic art

12 Sculpture from the Hindu-Javanese Kingdoms in Indonesia
13–14 Japanese section: screens, paintings, lacquerwork; wooden Amida statue (12th c.)
15–16 Arts and crafts of China; large sculptures, including grave figures from the T'ang period
17 East Asian sculpture; bronze statue of the god Shiva
19–22 Early Chinese ceramics and porcelain (c. 2000–1900 B.C.)

BASEMENT – Sculpture and decorative art

24 Dutch and foreign 18th c. glassware
25 Dutch Louis XVI furniture
27 Original furnishings from a house in Haarlem
28 Dutch porcelain: Weesp, Loosdrecht, Amstel and The Hague
29 Furniture from the Empire period; silverware
30 French and Dutch 18th c. costumes
31 18th and 19th c. lace
32 Dutch porcelain
33 Empire
34 Art Nouveau

Study collection

40 Sculpture and decorative arts
43 History, sculpture and decorative arts
47 Paintings

exhaustive account of the development of art and culture in the Netherlands and is especially rich in old Dutch handicrafts, medieval Dutch sculpture and modern Dutch paintings. The National Museum is divided into several departments, of which only the department exhibiting the work of Dutch masters of the 17th c. is always open. The other departments can be visited alternately in the morning or the afternoon from approximately 1 p.m. Details can be obtained by telephone.

Painting

The painting department houses an outstanding collection of Dutch 15th to 19th c. masters (especially those of the 17th c., the heyday of Dutch painting). Frans Hals, Johannes Vermeer, Jan Steen, Pieter de Hooch, Peter Paul Rubens and, of course, Rembrandt are represented here by their greatest works. Non-Dutch painters are grouped according to country; this collection includes such masters as Fra Angelico, Goya and Murillo.

Only the most important of the great number of masterpieces can be mentioned here. The most outstanding picture is Rembrandt's "Night Watch", restored after it was slashed in 1975, which is one of the master's largest and most famous compositions (1642); also by Rembrandt are the "Anatomy Lesson of Dr Deijman", the "Staalmeesters", the "Jewish Bride" and the portrait (1634) of the wife of the Rotterdam brewer, Haesje Cleyburg.

Frans Hals is represented by several lively portraits, including the "Merry Drinker" and the picture of the Civic Guard completed by Pieter Codde.

Jan Steen is shown not only as a humorist, with several accomplished paintings, but as a religious painter with his "Christ at Emmaus" and "Adoration of the Shepherds".

Gerhard ter Borch and Gabriel Metsu are also represented, as is Pieter de Hooch with his most outstanding works.

Among the museum's most precious treasures are the works of Jan Vermeer van Delft, including his "Straatje".

The "Mill at Wijk bij Duurstede" by Jacob Ruisdael is the most outstanding landscape.

The 17th c. Flemish painters are represented by Rubens (sketch for the "Crucifixion") and several portraits by Anthony van Dyck.

Among the Italian painters are Crivelli, Bellini and Mantegna, Veronese, Tintoretto and Bassano; and the Spanish painters include Velázquez ("Still Life"), Murillo ("Annunciation", "Madonna and Child"), Cano and Cerezo.

The SW annex contains the collection of later Dutch paintings which, in conjunction with the Stedelijk Museum (see entry), covers the whole range of Dutch 19th c. painting.

Print room

The print room specialises in Dutch 16th and 17th c. and French 18th c. drawings and prints. In the library the visitor can be shown all the prints from the national collection, such as Rembrandt's etchings.

Rijksmuseum: the most important art museum in Amsterdam ▶

Dutch history

This department displays paintings, model ships, flags, costumes, documents, curios and other items illustrating the political and military history of the Netherlands (altogether about 3000 exhibits). The exhibition is not a chronological account but highlights interrelated topics (which are in chronological order) of fundamental importance in the country's history.
The period covered ranges from the late Middle Ages to the present.

Sculpture and handicrafts

The wide-ranging exhibition of liturgical robes, furniture, tapestries, jewellery, pottery, costumes, dolls' houses, Delft pottery, lace, snuff boxes, etc. presents a picture of life in various periods from the Middle Ages to the early 20th c.

Oriental art

The visitor can see Chinese porcelain and objets d'art from India, South-East Asia and the Far East. Japanese prints are to be found in the print room.

Schiphol Airport (Luchthaven Schiphol)

Location
10 km (6 miles) SW (E10)

Buses
Shuttle service from the central station

From Oct. 1986 direct rail link from Centraal Station, then withdrawal of shuttle service.

Schiphol airport is 10 km (6 miles) SW of Amsterdam in the middle of the reclaimed Haarlemmermeer polder, about 4 m (13 ft) below sea level. Charts of 1610 term this area "Shipp Holl" which implies that many ships must have foundered here when it was the Haarlemmermeer.
Schiphol was first used by military aeroplanes for take-off and landing in 1917. In 1920 KLM started flights to London and thus brought Schiphol into the international air traffic network. On 10 May 1940 Schiphol was destroyed by bombing but soon after the war it was rebuilt and extended.

Schiphol: a "signpost" shows the distances to all the flight destinations

Nowadays over 85 airlines fly from Schiphol to more than 185 destinations in 90 countries. The airport complex includes five runways, arrival and departure buildings, radar installations and workshops. It ranks seventh among the European airports in terms of passengers (18 million a year) and fourth in terms of freight (438,162 tonnes a year).
There are magnificent viewing facilities with good views of all the runways on the roof of the 370 m (405 yd) long and 18 m (20 yd) wide central concourse where passengers board their planes. Part of this walk-way is covered. There are also good views from the comfort of the "Aviorama" restaurant.
Visitors to Schiphol should also take a look at the "Aviodrome" aviation museum (see Practical Information, Museums).
Seasoned air-travellers often make a detour via Schiphol to take advantage of one of the best and cheapest duty-free shops in Europe (40,000 different articles).

Schreierstoren (Wailing tower) C2

Location
On the corner of Prins Hendrikkade and Geldersekade

Buses
22, 46, 55, 56

On the corner of Prins Hendrikkade and Geldersekade, near the main station (see Centraal Station), stands the Wailing Tower, a fragment of the medieval city wall. It was the office of the harbour-master until 1960 when he moved into the Port Administration building. The tower has stood empty since that time.
There is some controversy about the real meaning of the name: a gable stone bearing the date 1569 shows a woman crying which gave rise to the idea that this was where the sailors' wives took leave of their husbands when they were about to go back to sea. A second version suggests that the name stems from the fact that the tower stands astride (schrijlings) a wall called the Kamperhoofd. In 1927 a bronze plaque was placed on the tower to commemorate Henry Hudson who set off from here on 4 April 1609 in his ship "De halve Maan" (Half Moon) on a journey which was to end in the founding of New Amsterdam (New York).

Singel H5/6 (A2–4/B1–2, 4)

Location
Between Herengracht and Voorburgswal

The Singel was originally a moat, and the city wall ran where the odd-numbered houses now stand. On the other side of the wall lay Amsterdam's vegetable gardens and meadows (the Torensluis is one of the former passages to the gardens). When the city was enlarged and the wall lost its defensive function, it was demolished (*c.* 1600) and houses were built on the site.
A walk along this canal is interesting because of the quaint details that emerge: No. 7 is no wider than a front door and is thus the narrowest house in Amsterdam. The bridge at the corner of the Oude Leliestraat has a cell just above water-level where men and women must have been put (separately) to sober up. Of particular architectural interest are Nos. 140–142, designed by the famous architect Hendrik de Keyser. Banning Cocq, the principal figure in Rembrandt's "Night Watch", lived here for a while. Finally, not far from the "Temple of Wisdom", the university library, there is the Amsterdam flower market, part of it on houseboats. (See Practical Information, Markets).

Stedelijk Museum

GROUND FLOOR

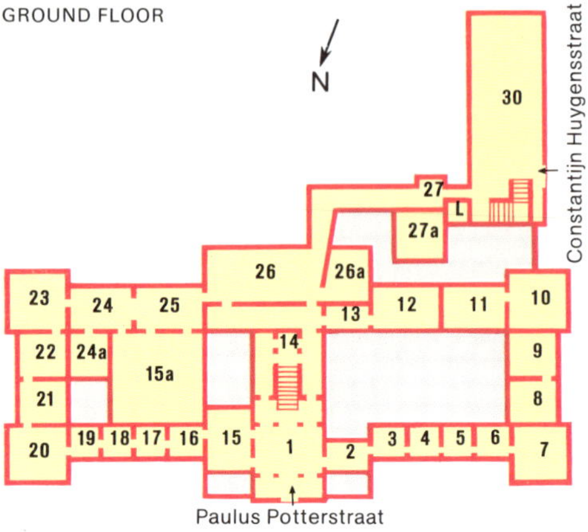

GROUND FLOOR
1 Entrance Information
8–11 Temporarily closed
15 Cloakroom
15a Auditorium Lecture Theatre
26 Restaurant
24a/27a Toilets
30 New Wing Cloakroom

The **Stedelijk Museum** (Municipal Museum), founded in 1885, which developed from the *Sophia Augusta De Bruin* foundation, is a *modern art museum* (painting, sculpture, collages, environments, etc.). Only part of the extensive collection is on show at any one time.

Sophia Augusta De Bruin collection: Regency, Louis XV, Louis XVI and Empire interiors; 18th c. kitchen with Delft tiles. Barbizon school: Camille Corot, Charles Daubigny, Gustave Courbet, Honoré Daumier, Aimé Millet, Henri Fantin-Latour, Johann Barthold Jongkind, George Hendrik Breitner, Henri de Toulouse-Lautrec, Edgar Degas, Edouard Manet, Odilon Redon, Paul Gauguin, Paul Cézanne, Claude Monet, James Ensor, Maurice de Vlaminck, Kees van Dongen, Fernand Léger, Edouard Vuillard, Pierre Bonnard, Pablo Picasso, Georges Rouault, Chaim Soutine, Georges Braque, Gino Severini, Raoul Dufy, Elie Delaunay, Marc Chagall, Vassily Kandinski, Ernst Ludwig Kirchner, Oskar Kokoschka, Lovis Corinth, Max Pechstein, August Macke, Paul Klee. De Stijl: Piet Mondrian, Theo van Doesburg. Cobra: Karel Appel, Corneille, Asger Jorn, Pierre Alechinsky, Max Ernst. Action Painting: Jackson Pollock. Pop Art: Roy Lichtenstein, Robert Rauschenberg, Allen Jones, Victor de Vasarely, George Segal, Edward Kienholz. Mobiles by Alexander Calder

FIRST FLOOR

SECOND FLOOR

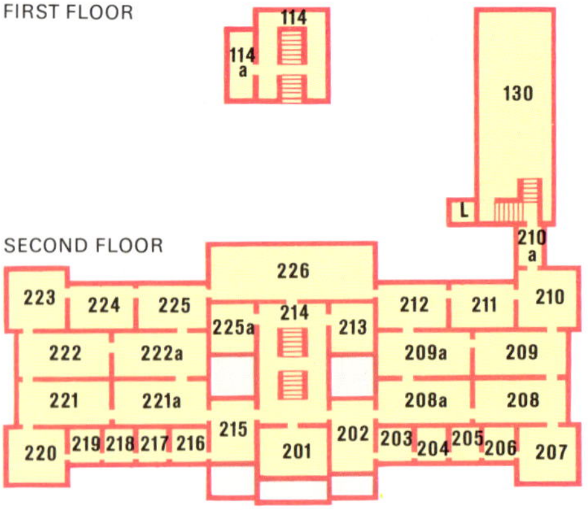

FIRST FLOOR
114 Print room (engravings)
114a Print department study room
130 New Wing

SECOND FLOOR
201 Sale of reproductions

L Lift

**Stedelijk Museum (Municipal Museum) G7

The Municipal Museum (founded in 1885) is one of Europe's most important modern art museums. Its collection mainly covers 19th and 20th c. Dutch and French painting.
The museum owes its existence to the appreciation of art and the generosity of leading citizens of Amsterdam. Its collection is based on the gift of the widow Suasso-De Bruin ("Sophia Augusta foundation"). Chr. P. van Eeghen's collection of contemporary art was added to this as well as other collections not confined to contemporary works. These were later transferred to other museums, since in accordance with its original concept the Municipal Museum specialises in modern art from the mid-19th c. onwards.

Location
Paulus Potterstraat 13

Trams
2, 5, 16

Times of opening
Daily 11 a.m.–5 p.m.

Guided tours in English
By arrangement

Admission fee

The following are some of the movements and artists represented:
De Stijl (Van Doesburg, Mondrian, Rietveld), Cobra (Karel Appel, Corneille, Jorn), Colourfield Painting (Kelly, Louis, Newman), Pop Art (Rosenquist, Warhol), Nouveau Réalisme (Armand, Spoerri, Tinguely); painters such as Chagall, Dubuffet, De Kooning, Malevitch and Matisse.
The sculpture garden contains numerous works, including those of Rodin, Moore, Renoir, Woulers, Laurens, Serra and Visser.
The Municipal Museum has its own library and puts on avant-garde films, concerts and exhibitions.

The Stedelijk Museum's new premises

Stedelijk Museum: exhibition room

Theater Carré J6

Location
Amstel 115–125

Telephone
22 52 25

Trams
4, 9

When Amsterdam lost its fair, Oscar Carré, director of the Carré Circus which was exceedingly popular at the turn of the century, began to look for a permanent site in Amsterdam. He found a suitable spot on the Amstel and obtained a temporary permit to build a wooden marquee. However, he ignored the official requirements and had a stone roof put on his marquee. When the municipality ordered him to demolish it he applied for a permanent permit. Eventually he met with success and the Carré in the form we know it today was opened in 1887.

After Oscar Carré's death in 1911 it was converted into a theatre, but this was not as successful as the circus, and in the end the Carré family had to sell the building. It changed hands several times before being transferred in 1927 to a company whose manager, Alex Wunnink, succeeded in re-establishing its importance in Amsterdam's theatre life.

Today all kinds of artistes appear here, plus ballets, musicals and circuses.

Trippenhuis (Trip house) C3

Location
Kloveniersburgwal 29

The elegant mansion, on the corner of the Amstel and the Nieuwmarkt (see entry), was built by the Trip brothers (immensely rich cannon manufacturers) and today houses the Dutch Academy of Sciences.

When the two "cannon kings" moved to Amsterdam they wanted an imposing house to live in. In 1662 they were able to move into the "Trip house" and the chimneys are shaped like the mortars to which the brothers owed their wealth.

Metro
Nieuwmarkt

Buses
22, 25

Tradition has it that one of the family's servants was heard to say, "Oh, if only I had a house as wide as your front door I should be happy!" One of the Trip brothers overheard this and had a little house built of the same materials and in the same style opposite the Trip house. This little Trip house is still there today at No. 26.

The Royal Institute for Science, Literature and Fine Arts, today the Dutch Academy of Sciences, moved into the Trip house in 1808.

*Tropenmuseum (Tropical Museum) K6

The Tropical Museum, with its exhibition of artistic and everyday objects from tropical and subtropical regions, is part of the Royal Tropical Institute. Here one can wander through a bazaar, look inside Far Eastern houses and be amazed to find that even in the Far East shops sell bottles of Coca Cola. The Tropical Museum also has a children's workshop, regular concerts of oriental and asiatic music and an extensive library (see also Practical Information, Libraries – Tropical Institute Library and Museums).

Location
Linnaeusstraat 2

Bus
22

Trams
3, 6, 8, 10

Times of opening
Mon.–Fri. 10 a.m.–5 p.m.; Sat., Sun. and public holidays noon–5 p.m.

Closed
1 Jan., 30 Apr., 25 Dec.

The original purpose of the Royal Tropical Institute, successor to the "Koloniaal Instituut", was to disseminate information about the Dutch colonies (Surinam, Indonesia and the Dutch West Indies). Nowadays, however, it concentrates on the problems of the Third World. Admission fee.

Universiteit van Amsterdam (University) A3

The Amsterdam Municipal University, endowed in 1877 and therefore comparatively young, was the first university in the Netherlands after the war to set up a faculty of social and political sciences. It has the reputation of being progressive, and distinguished itself at the time of the student unrest and the "Provo" period in the mid-sixties by its political activities. One of the main university buildings is the former old people's home on the Oudemanhuispoort (see entry).

Location
Spui

Trams
1, 2

The "Vrije Universiteit", opened in 1880, is a Christian-oriented university in which teaching is based on the Reformed faith.

**Van Gogh Museum (officially: Rijksmuseum Vincent van Gogh) G7

The biggest Van Gogh collection in the world (a donation from Van Gogh's brother Theo and his nephew V. W. Van Gogh), formerly in the Stedelijk Museum (see entry), has been housed since 1972 in the museum specially built for it by Gerrit Rietveld. The collection consists of around 200 paintings, 500

Location
Paulus Potterstraat 7

Trams
2, 5, 16

Times of opening
Tues.–Sat. 10 a.m.–5 p.m.; Sun. and public holidays 1–5 p.m.

Closed
1 Jan. and Mon.

drawings and 700 letters. There are also works by those of Van Gogh's contemporaries who influenced him or were influenced by him (including Gauguin and Toulouse-Lautrec). The extensive library contains literature on Vincent Van Gogh and his times. Courses (e.g. photography, painting and various printing techniques) are held in the workshop attached to the museum. Admission fee.

*Vlooienmarkt (officially: Waterlooplein; flea market) C3

Location
Valkenburgerstraat

Metro
Waterlooplein

Bus
56

Tram
9

Times of opening
Mon.–Sat. 10 a.m.–4 p.m.

"Whether there are fleas in the flea market in Amsterdam is hard to say; there is certainly everything else. Threadbare clothes, once the height of fashion, and factory surplus lie side by side waiting for buyers, to be gaped at, smiled at, scoffed at: unsold." This is one writer's description of the scene on the Waterlooplein (see Jodenbuurt) where dealers large and small offer their wares for sale on stalls or simply on the ground – a colourful jumble of junk and utilities and a tatty treasure trove.
The flea market had to move because of the construction of the underground, the new town hall and the Opera House. Now smaller, it is round the corner in Valkenburgerstraat where the stalls are permanent and the dealers store their goods away in container lorries overnight. The old picturesque atmosphere has suffered somewhat, but the flea market continues to attract visitors from home and abroad.
Anyone who looks long enough can still find old domestic utensils, books, etc. at reasonable prices, although pictures and the like are not as cheap as they used to be.

Volendam: fishermen by the harbour

*Volendam

Location
20 km (12 miles) NE (E10)

Buses
Stop outside Centraal Station (NZH bus)

VVV
See Practical Information, Information

The village of Volendam in North Holland is part of the district of Edam-Volendam (see Edam) and lies on the IJsselmeer. As elsewhere, its fishing industry has been hard hit by the damming of the Zuider Zee (see entry).

Volendam is the Catholic counterpart of Marken (see entry). It is famous in the Netherlands for its folk costumes so that it is not surprising that tourism has become its main source of income. The older inhabitants still wear their costumes with pride: for the men this consists of baggy woollen breeches, while the women wear flowered dresses with striped aprons, coral necklaces, and in cold weather blue-and-white-striped shawls. During the week the women usually wear a simple cheesecloth cap, but on Sundays and holidays this is replaced by the famous lace headdress. From Volendam boat excursions can be made to Marken and Monnickendam. The young people prefer modern dress.
Besides the harbour and the picturesque old houses the following are of interest:
The wooden church dating from 1685 (restored 1955).
The collection of paintings in the Hotel Spaander by the harbour, with more than 100 works by old masters.
Volendam Museum (Kloostervuurt 5), open daily in summer from 10 a.m. to 5 p.m.
"De Gouden Kamer" (Oude Draaipad 8) which is papered with millions of cigar bands assembled to make pictures such as New York's Statue of Liberty.
In Slobbeland it is possible to see how the houses used to be built on piles.

Times of opening
Daily in summer
9 a.m.–6 p.m.

Vondelpark F/G7

Location
Main entrance: Leidseplein

Trams
1, 2, 3, 6, 12

This green lung in the heart of Amsterdam is named after Joost van den Vondel, Holland's most famous poet (see General Information, Famous People). His statue was unveiled in the park in 1867. The park, Amsterdam's Bois de Boulogne as one newspaper called it when it was opened, covers approximately 48 hectares (119 acres) and is landscaped on English lines, with sandpits and playgrounds, ponds and fountains, flower-beds and lawns, a rose-garden and a little tea-house, a number of different trees and hedges providing homes for many birds.
At the time of the "Provos" in the mid-sixties the Vondelpark was inhabited by hippies, but when drug-pushing and such attendant crimes as theft became rife, the authorities decided to forbid sleeping in the park at night (see Practical Information, Drugs).
During the summer the park is the venue for the Vondelpark Festival and many other programmes of music, drama and children's events.

Waaggebouw (Weigh-house) C2

Location
Nieuwmarkt 4

The old weigh-house with its seven towers in the Nieuwmarkt (see entry) is the former St Anthony's Gate (St Antoniepoort),

Metro
Nieuwmarkt

Buses
22, 55

once part of the 15th c. city wall. With the growth of the city it was converted in 1617 into the weigh-house and was used to weigh ships' anchors and ordnance as well as foodstuffs.
The upper floor served as the guildhall. Each guild (painters, smiths, surgeons, etc.) had its own entrance. The guild of stonemasons was responsible for its internal and external decoration; the chamber of the guild of bricklayers has been kept in its original state.
In the 17th c. the surgeons gave their lectures on anatomy here and their entrance can still be recognised today by the inscription "Theatrum Anatomicum" above the doorway. Rembrandt was a frequent guest at these lectures which inspired him to paint his "Anatomy Lesson of Dr Tulp" (Mauritshuis, The Hague) and "Anatomy Lesson of Dr Deijman" (Rijksmuseum).
It was this use that ultimately saved the weigh-house from demolition, since the surgeons needed the building for their work. After 1819 the weigh-house was used for several purposes, including use as a fire-station, for municipal archives and as a museum (see Amsterdams Historisch Museum).

Museum of Jewish History

Times of opening
Tues.–Sat. 10 a.m.–5 p.m.;
Sun. and public holidays
1–5 p.m.

Admission fee

The Joods Historische Museum in the weigh-house was set up in 1925. In 1940 the collection of objects connected with the Jewish religion and the daily life of the Jewish community was carried off to Germany but the museum was reopened in 1955 with almost all its former exhibits. The exhibition is completed by material on the German Occupation. In addition temporary exhibitions are mounted. The library has a stock of 5000 volumes.
Since the Museum is due to move in 1987, it is closing from November 1986 to May 1987. Already parts of the collection are no longer on view. The VVV will provide information about the reopening in the new location.

Walletjes B/C2/3

In the oldest part of Amsterdam, between the O.Z. Voorburgwal and the Achterburgwal (see entry), in the triangle formed by the central station, the Dam and the Nieuwmarkt, lie "de Walletjes", the red light district. The "oldest profession" was officially sanctioned here as far back as the 14th c. Along the romantic canals and in the small side alleys the prostitutes sit in their "shop-windows" and offer themselves for sale. If the red light is out and the curtains are drawn the ladies are busy.

"De Walletjes" seem strangely sedate with their bizarre mixture of scantily clad girls, sex-shops and little old lady shopkeepers, tourists and locals (not all of whom are clients by any means). Visitors should beware of pickpockets.

*Westerkerk (West Church) G5/6

Location
Prinsengracht/corner of
Raadhuisstraat
Buses
14, 21, 67

The Westerkerk, in which the magnificent wedding of Princess (now Queen) Beatrix to Claus von Amsberg took place in 1966, is the most popular church in the city. Its tower, popularly known as "Langer Jan" (tall John), which at 85 m (279 ft) is the highest in the city, serves as a symbol of Amsterdam.

After the town went over to Protestantism Hendrick de Keyser began the building in 1620 of the Renaissance church which, uncharacteristically, has many internal and external Gothic features.

After de Keyser's death the building was completed in 1630 by Jacob van Campen, and the tower added. On the tip of the spire is the emperor's crown, in memory of Emperor Maximilian of Austria who, in 1489, was cured of an illness in Amsterdam and gave the city his protection and the right to include his crown in its coat of arms. A carillon inside the tower proclaims the hours. Its hammer weighs 200 kg (440 lb) and the largest of the 48 bells weighs 7500 kg ($3\frac{3}{4}$ tons).

The church was consecrated in 1631 with a Whitsun service. The people of the surrounding Jordaan district (see entry) stayed away at first because of the upper classes from along the canals who came here to worship. They wanted a church of their own which they finally acquired with the Noorderkerk.

Besides a fine organ (1622) the church contains an interesting marble column placed there in 1906 in memory of Rembrandt. Rembrandt, who died in poverty, was initially buried outside the church. He was only subsequently reinterred inside the church and his (probably empty) grave is in its northern section (see also Rembrandthuis).

Trams
13, 17

Times of opening
Church: 1 Apr.–15 Sept., Mon.–Sat. 10 a.m.–4 p.m.
Tower: 1 June–15 Sept., Tues., Wed., Fri., Sat. 2–5 p.m.

*Zaanse Schans

About 15 km (9 miles) out of Amsterdam one comes across a little piece of "picture-book Holland": the **reconstruction** of a Zaanland village as it would have looked **about the year** 1700.

Location
Zaanstad, 15 km (9 miles) NW (A8)

Westerkerk: its tower serves as a symbol of Amsterdam

Rail
From Centraal Station to Koog-Zaandijk Station on the Alkmaar line, then 8 min. walk

Times of opening
1 Apr.–1 Nov.: daily 9 a.m.–5 p.m.; Winter: Sat., Sun. 9 a.m.–5 p.m.

Information
See Practical Information, Information, VVV Zaandam

This open-air museum was privately set up in 1948. The Zaanse Schans Foundation managed to rescue old buildings that stood in the way of industrial expansion and typical 17th and 18th c. wooden houses and windmills were dismantled to be re-erected here.
That this open-air museum gives the visitor such a true-to-life picture of the past is due in no small measure to the fact that almost all of the carefully restored houses are inhabited.
At the beginning of the 18th c. this area had about 500 Dutch windmills. Half of them ground mustard, oil, cocoa, spices and tobacco as well as flour. The other half were saw-mills, since the timber industry had been very important in this area in the 17th c. Among the few mills still maintained in Zaanse Schans a dye-mill, a mustard-mill and a sawmill can be visited; there are also a cheese-dairy, an old bakery, an old grocery, a clog-maker's and a pewterer's, as well as the Zaans Museum of Clock-making (Zaanse Uurwerken Museum) with a collection of old Dutch clocks. The old houses and windmills form a delightful backdrop to a boat trip on the Zaans.

Zaanstad

Buses
ENHABO bus (stop opposite Centraal Station)

The various places on the river Zaan together make up the town and district of Zaanstad.

Zaandam

VVV
See Practical Information, Information

Tsar Peter the Great of Russia worked here for four months in 1697 unrecognised, under the name of Peter Michael, as a carpenter and a shipwright. Reminders of that time are the Tsar Peter House (Krimp 24) and the Tsar Peter Monument on the Dam presented to the town by Tsar Nicholas II in 1911.
Places worth seeing: the Old Catholic Church, 1695 (Papenpad 12), the old saw-mill "Held Josua" (behind the station) and the "Ooievaar", a water-mill dating from 1640 (on the S side of the Julia bridge).

Zaandijk

Times of opening
Tues.–Fri. 10 a.m.–noon, 2–4 p.m., Sun. 2–4 p.m.

The Zaanlandse Oudheidkamer (Lagedijk 80), with its exhibition of toys, costumes, ship models and other 17th and 18th c. objects, is well worth a visit. There is also the Weefhuis (weaving house) or "House with the Picture Garden" (Lagedjik 39), the corn-mill called "Death", built in 1656 (Lagedjik 28; open every third Saturday in the month from 2 to 5 p.m.) and the Stadhuis (town hall; Lagedjik 104), an old merchant's house; its beautiful interior, however, is not shown to visitors.

Koog aan de Zaan

Times of opening
Tues.–Fri. 10 a.m.–noon, 2–5 p.m., Sat., Sun. 2–5 p.m.

The Mill Museum (Moolenmuseum at Museumslaan 18) provides an interesting survey of 17th and 18th c. mills using scale models and documents. A visit to the old oil mill of 1610, "Het Pink" (in Pinkstraat), completes the picture. this belongs to the Moolenmuseum, Zaanse Schans (for times of opening see that entry).

Westzaan

Times of opening
July and Aug.: Tues.–Sat. 9.30 a.m.–5 p.m.; otherwise Mon.–Fri. 9.30 a.m.–5 p.m.

Places of interest: the Great Church (Torenstraat) with temporary exhibitions in July and August; "Het Prinsenhof" (Weelsloot), a mill of 1722 (open Apr.–Oct. on the third Saturday in the month, 2 to 5 p.m.) and "De Schoolmeester" (Guisweg), built in 1695, the only paper-mill in the world which is still working. The Stadhuis (Kerkbuurt), a former court-house with a cupola in the style of Louis XIV, is not open to the public, but the unusually fine interior furnishing of the Zuidervermaning Church (Zuideinde 231) can be seen on application to the sacristan who lives near by.

De Rijp

The birthplace of J. A. Leeghwater, the inventor of the diving bell (1575–1650).

VVV
See Practical Information, Information

Times of opening
Easter–Oct.: Sat., Sun. 11 a.m.–5 p.m. June–Aug.: Fri.–Mon. 10 a.m.–5 p.m.

Places of interest:
The Houten Huis Museum (Jan Boonplein 2), with displays of tiles, ceramics, old sea-charts and the skeleton of a whale.
The Waagegebouw (weigh-house) at Kleine Dam 2, which dates from 1690, has 24 stained-glass windows of 1655. It can be visited by arrangement with the VVV.

Purmerend

VVV
See Practical Information, Information

Purmerend has been an important market town since 1484. The cheese-market, held every Tuesday 11 a.m. to 1 p.m. from July to September, is interesting. Also worth a visit is the Koepelkerk in the Kaasmarkt, with its famous Garrels church organ; this can be seen by arrangement (tel. 02990/32205). It is now a cultural centre.

Broek in Waterland

Broek in Waterland is one of the prettiest Dutch villages. The little settlement consists of 18th c. wooden houses grouped around a large pond. There are still two cheese-makers and a clog-maker here.

Zandvoort

Location
25 km (16 miles) W (A5, A9)

Buses
Stop at Marnixstraat

VVV
See Practical Information, Information

Zandvoort is in North Holland on the North Sea and is internationally known as one of the most important Dutch seaside resorts. It has over 1½ million overnight visitors a year. It is also famous for its 4·2 km (2·625 mile) long motor and motor-cycle Grand Prix circuit (opened in 1948).
Although it has all the attractions of a modern seaside resort Zandvoort has tried to preserve its old character, and the renovation of the northern part of the town has sought to retain the atmosphere of the old fishing village which, until 1828, had only 700 inhabitants. The Folklore Association and the Old Zandvoort Society also try to maintain the old customs and traditional costumes.
Besides the sea and the broad beaches Zandvoort's other attractions include:
The 60 m (197 ft) high observation tower with restaurant.
The "Dolfirama" dolphinarium with dolphins and sealions (at Burgermeester van Fenemaplien 2; at present closed. Information from VVV).

Times of opening
Mon.–Sat. 2 p.m.–2 a.m.

Closed
Apr. and May

The Zandvoort casino (Badhuisplatz 7) on the eighteenth floor of "Bouwes" is the highest point on the Dutch coast.
To be able to gamble one must be at least 18 years old. Correct attire is required. Visitors are registered, therefore a passport or driving licence should not be forgotten. One can try one's luck at the roulette table for a stake of 5, 10 or 20 guilders, and at blackjack for a stake of 5 or 10 guilders.

Zoo

See Artis

Zandvoort: seaside resort on Amsterdam's doorstep

*Zuider Zee

Originally the Zuider Zee was a bay in the North Sea. After it was cut off by the Afsluitdijk in 1932 its name was changed to the IJsselmeer. The plan was to reclaim some of the land for industry and agriculture and for use as residential areas. Some of the polders, as the reclaimed areas are called, are already in use: the Wieringermeer polder, covering 20,000 hectares (49,420 acres) was reclaimed as early as 1930; the Noordoostpolder (1942) covers 48,000 hectares (118,608 acres), and the reclamation of the East Flevoland polder (54,000 hectares – 133,434 acres) and the South Flevoland polder (44,000 hectares – 108,724 acres) was completed in 1957 and 1968 respectively.

Lelystad in East Flevoland is to become a residential and industrial centre of national importance.

There are plans to build the towns of Almere and Zeewolde in South Flevoland. The primary objective of these polders and of the Markerwaard which has yet to be reclaimed is to reduce the pressure of population on the surrounding conurbations. They will be residential, employment and recreational areas. The remaining lakes around the edges are becoming the sites of swimming pools, camp-sites and marinas. Last but not least, the polders enable important lines of communication to be set up – for example, between the provinces of North Holland and Friesland.

Visitors who are interested in the land-reclamation project should visit the Enkhuizen Zuidersee Museum (see Practical Information, Museums concerning land-reclamation).

Practical Information A–Z

Advance Booking

Stadsshouwburg, UIT Bureau (AUB) and Leidseplein 26 advance ticket sales for all musical events, plays, ballets, etc. in Amsterdam. Free monthly programme of events
Open: Mon.–Sat. 10 a.m.–6 p.m.

Trams 1, 2, 5

Theater Bespreek Bureau
Stationsplein 10 (opposite Centraal Station)
Open Mon.–Sat. 10 a.m.–4 p.m.

VVV

Airlines (Luchtvaartmaatschappij)

KLM
Leidseplein 1. Tel. 47 47 74 7

Air UK
Postbus/PO Box 12010
3004 GA Rotterdam
Tel. (010) 37 02 11

Australian Airways/Qantas
Rokin 9. Tel. 25 50 15

Canadian Pacific
Leidsestraat 55. Tel. 22 44 44

Pan Am
Leidseplein 31c. Tel. 26 20 21

SAA/SAL
Stadhouderskade 2. Tel. 16 44 44

Airport (Luchthaven)

Amsterdam airport is appr. 12 km (7 miles) SW of the city near the E10 motorway from Amsterdam to The Hague. From October 1986 a direct rail link runs from the Centraal Station to the airport. The existing bus service to the inner city is suspended. Telephone General 5110432; Charter 5110666

Schiphol

Antiques

Amsterdam has a great many antique shops in Nieuwe Spiegelstraat, Spiegelgracht, Rohin, Elandsgracht and elsewhere in the city. Prices are much the same as in any other European capital.

Shops

A selection:
Amsterdam Antiques Gallery,
Nieuwe Spiegelstraat 34

A. van de Meer
P.C. Hooftstraat 112
Fine prints

Premsela en Hamburger
Rokin 120
Jewellery, gold and silver

E. Wassenaar
Hobbemastraat 10a
Jewellery

1900–1930
Keizersgracht 347
Art nouveau

Ingrid Vos
Lijnbaansgracht 290
Art nouveau

Markets

"De Looier" antiques market
Elandsgradet 109
Tram: 17
Open: Mon.–Thurs. 11 a.m.–5 p.m., Sat. 9 a.m.–5 p.m.

Flea Markets

See Markets

Nieuwmarkt

An antiques and secondhand goods market takes place on the Nieuwmarkt from the middle of May until the end of September.

Arrival

Room Reservation

Visitors arriving in Amsterdam who have not booked a room and who are not members of an organised tour or group should apply to the Tourist Bureau (see Information).

Young People

For years Amsterdam has been a Mecca for young people; therefore there is a wide choice of inexpensive accommodation: camp sites, youth hostels, "sleep-ins" and student hotels (sse Hotels, Inexpensive Accommodation). For advice and assistance by the tourist bureau see Information.

Warning

Sleeping in the Vondelpark or in a car is no longer allowed.

Advancing Booking

See Arrival in Amsterdam.

Auction Houses (Veilingen)

The following auction houses handle antiques, furniture, objets d'art and books:

Paul Brandt, Keizersgracht 738
De Eland, Elandsgracht 68
Sotheby, Rokin 102
De Zwaan, Keizersgracht 474
Christies, Cornelis Schuytstraat 57

Banks

Australia

Commonwealth Trading Bank of Australia
c/o ABN Bank
P.O. Box 669
Tel. 29 91 11

Canada

Canadian Imperial Bank of Commerce
Uijzelstraat 79/b/u
Tel. 22 93 97

South Africa

South African Bank
c/o Barclays International Ltd
P.O. Box 160
Tel. 26 22 09

United Kingdom

Standard Chartered Bank Ltd
Herengracht 418
Tel. 26 22 09

United States of America

Bank of America
Keizersgracht 617
Tel. 21 46 21

Times of Opening

Mon.–Fri. 9 a.m.–4 p.m.
Some banks open until 7 p.m. on days when the shops stay open late.

The Algemene Bank Nederland at Schiphol airport is open every day from 7 a.m. until midnight.

Travellers' Cheques

Eurocheques and Travellers' Cheques are exchanged at all banks

Exchange Offices

Outside normal business hours money can be exchanged at the following banks:
GWK:
Main Station: Mon.–Sat. 7 a.m.–10.45 p.m., Sun. 8 a.m.–10.45 p.m.
Amstel Station: Mon.–Sat. 8 a.m.–8 p.m. Sun. 10 a.m.–4 p.m.
KML House, Leidseplein: Mon.–Fri. 8.30 a.m.– 5.30 p.m., Sat. 10 a.m.–2 p.m.
Schiphol Airport: Mon.–Sat. 8 a.m.–8 p.m., Sun. 10 a.m.–4 p.m.

Change Express Exchange Office:
Damrak 17: daily 8 a.m.–midnight
Damrak 86: daily 8 a.m.–11.45 p.m.
Kalverstraat 150: daily 8 a.m.–8 p.m.
Leidsestraat 106: daily 8 a.m.–midnight

Thomas Cook Exchange Office:
Dam 23–25: daily 8.30 a.m.–10 p.m.
Leidseplein 31a: daily 8.30 a.m.–10 p.m.
Damrak 20: daily 8.30 a.m.–10 p.m.

Baths

Anyone who is not satisfied with the hygenic arrangements in his accommodation, can take advantage of public baths. These are excellently run and are comparatively inexpensive. Addresses are:

Andreas Bonnstraat 28
Marnixplein 9
Da Costakade 200
1e Sweenlinckstraat 10
For opening times apply to VVV (See Information). Baths are closed on Sunday and Monday.

Bicycle Hire (Fietsverkuur)

There is hardly any more original and comfortable way of discovering Amsterdam than on a bicycle, although bikes are quite expensive to hire. The following shops hire out the famous "Dutch bicycles" on a daily or weekly basis:

Fiets-O-Fiets, Amstelveenseweg 880–900. Tel. 44 54 73, Buses: CN 170, 171, 172
Heja, Bestevaerstraat 39. Tel. 12 92 11, Tram: 13
Koenders, Utrechtsedwarsstraat 105. Tel. 23 46 57, Tram: 4
Koenders Rent-a-bike, Stationsplein Oostzijde. Tel. 24 83 91, Trams: 1, 2, 4, 5, 8, 13, 16, 17, 24, 25

Bookshops (Boekwinkel)

Nearly all Dutch bookshops sell the original English-language versions of English and American books.

English Bookshop Club
Leidsestraat 52

Athenaeum
Spui 14
Books and magazines

Erasmus
Spui 2
Art books

van Gennep
Nes 128
Books on politics

Allert de Lange
Damrak 62
Literature and travel guides

Book Market

Oudemanhuispoort – see A–Z

Breakdown Service

Automobile Club

The ANWB Dutch automobile club offers the same services as the English automobile clubs.

ANWB

Museumplein 5. Tel. 73 08 44
Open: Mon.–Fri. 8.45 a.m.–4.15 p.m., Sat. 8.45 a.m.–noon

Breakdown Service

In the event of a breakdown it is possible to call in the ANWB patrol service ("Wegenwacht") by ringing 26 82 51 which is manned daily from 7 a.m. until midnight. The service is free if the owner of the vehicle can produce an international automobile club membership card. Otherwise he will be assisted on payment of 45 guilders. A visitor who is not a member of a motoring organisation affiliated to the AIT (Alliance International de Tourisme) can nevertheless claim assistance by taking out temporary membership of the ANWB for a month (65 guilders in 1986).
Information about road conditions, traffic hold-ups and weather conditions can be obtained by telephoning the ANWB, Den Haag (Tel. 070 31 31 31; 24 hours a day including weekends).

Cafés

Dutch cafés have much in common with English pubs. Amsterdam is famous for its "brown cafés" (bruine kroegen), which get their name from their dark, tobacco-stained interiors.

A selection:

De Balle
Leidseplein
Open: from 4 p.m.
Rendezvous for artists from the De Balle Theatre, a former prison. Noted cuisine

De Engelsbewaarder
Kloveniersburgwal 59
Open: 11 a.m.–1 a.m.
Literary café; also talks and live music

Frascati
Nes 59
Open: Mon.–Sat. 10 a.m.–1 a.m. Sun. from 5 p.m.
Artists' café with theatrical events

Karperschoek
Martelaarsgracht 2
Open: Mon.–Fri. 7 a.m.–1 a.m. Sat. and Sun. 8 a.m.–1 a.m.
Oldest café in Amsterdam; very popular

Mulder
Weteringsschans 163
Open: 8.30 a.m.–1 a.m.
Genever (gin) from the barrel

De Prins
Prinsengracht 124
Open: 11 a.m.–1 a.m.
Café furnished like a drawing-room

Reijnders
Leidseplein 6
Open: 9 a.m.–1 a.m.
Artists' rendezvous with old interior

Schelteme
Nieuwe Zijdsvoorburgwal 242
Open: 8 a.m.–11 p.m.
Haunt of journalists

't Schmackzeyl
Brouwersgracht 101
Open: 9 a.m.–11 p.m.
Canal House

Welling
J. W. Brouwerstraat 32
Open: noon–1 a.m.
Living-room atmosphere

For Jazz fans

't Doktertje
Rozeboomsteg 4
Open: 4 p.m.–1 a.m.
Tiny café with good music

Bim Huis
Open: before and after jazz concerts; frequented by jazz fans and musicians

For Chess players

Schachcafé
Korte Leidsewartstraat
Open: 9 a.m.–midnight

Pleasant atmosphere

Hotel American
Leidseplein
Open: 9 a.m.–midnight

Bodega Keyzer
opposite the Concertgebouw
Open: 9 a.m.–midnight
Artists' rendezvous

Calendar of Events

January — Horecava: international fair for the hotel and catering trade

February — 25 February: commemoration of the strike in February 1941 by Dutch workers protesting against the deportation of their Jewish compatriots

March — Hiswa international watersport exhibition

April — 30 April: Koninginnedag (the Queen's Birthday). The whole city is in a festive mood with music and bring and buy sales, with everyone, including the children, joining in. 30 April was originally the birthday of Queen Juliana, and her daughter, Queen Beatrix, has kept the same date although her own birthday is in fact on 31 January

Also in April:
Ideal Home Exhibition
World Press Photo Exhibition, Nieuwe Kerk

May

4 May: Commemoration of those who died in the Second World War, with a two-minute silence at 8 p.m. throughout the Netherlands

5 May: Day of Liberation (the German Occupation ended on 5 May 1945), with local celebrations in various parts of the city

Saturday before Whitsun:
Luilak (literally "lazybones"), when children ring doorbells and make a lot of noise to wake up lie-a-beds and lazybones

Also in May:
Pasar Malam (Indonesian market)
Sunday Antiques Market on the Nieuwmarkt (until September)

June

Festival of Fools (in summer, in even numbered years)

Holland Festival (from June to August) Vondelpark Openluchttheater (open-air theatre): Children's theatre, music and dancing, etc.
Organ Recitals in Amsterdam Churches (until August)
Summer Evening Concerts in the Concertgebouw (until August)

Ballet Festival of the National Ballet
Summer Festival: Performances in Amsterdam's smaller theatres

September

1st Saturday in September:
Floral Procession from Aalsmeer to Amsterdam
Street Festival in the Jordaan quarter

November

3rd Saturday in November:
Entry of Saint Nicholas (Sinterklaas), who arrives by boat in front of the Centraal Station from "Spain" with his followers and, riding on a white horse, leads his procession through the city to the cathedral where he is welcomed by the Lord Mayor

Also in November:
Europoort Harbour Exhibition

December

5 December, Sinterklaas (Saint Nicholas Day celebrations): Public holiday when presents are exchanged as happens on Christmas Day in English-speaking countries

Kerstflora (Christmas flora)

Camp Sites

The camp sites in and around Amsterdam offer one of the cheapest forms of accommodation, which is generally expensive.

Amsterdamse IJSCLUB
IJsbaanpad 45. Tel. 62 09 16
Tram 16, 24 or night bus 71
Open: 15 March–1 October

Camping Vliegenbos
Meeuwenlaan 138. Tel. 36 88 55
Buses 32 or 33, change at stop after first tunnel from Central Station to bus 39 to terminal
Open: 1 April–30 September

Stichting Camping Zeeburg
Zuider IJdijk 44. Tel. 94 44 30
Open: beginning April–beginning October
Buses: 22 (Centraal Station), 37 (Muiderpoort) to Zeeburgdijk
Trams: 3 (Vondelpark), 10 (Leidseplein) to Flevoparkbad
Night bus: 71 (Centraal Station) to Zeeburgerdijk
July–August direct bus service from camp site to Centraal Station; tent hire

Camping Amsterdam Bos
Kleine Noorddijk 1, 1432 CC Aalsmeer. Tel. 020 41 68 68

Gaaspercamping
Loosdrechtdreef 7. Tel. 96 73 26

Car Hire

Cars

Ansa International
Apollolaan 138 (Hilton Hotel). Tel. 64 82 62

Avis
Keizersgracht 485. Tel. 26 22 01

Budget Rent-a-Car
Overtoom 121. Tel. 12 60 66

Diks
Van Ostadestraat, 278–280. Tel. 62 33 66

Europcar
Overtoom 51–53. Tel. 18 45 95

Hertz
Overtoom 333. Tel. 85 24 41

InterRent
Amstelveenseweg 294. Tel. 73 04 77

Kaspers en Lotte
Van Ostadestraat 232–234. Tel. 71 70 66

Kuperus BV
Middenweg 175. Tel. 93 87 90

Van Wijk European Car Rental Service
Schiphol. Tel. 17 24 05

Motor Caravans

Ansa International
Apollolaan 138–140. Tel. 64 82 62

Braitman & Woudenberg
Droogbak 4. Tel. 22 11 68

Auto Swart
Langestraat 14. Tel. 23 01 54

Diks
Generaal Vetterstraat 51–55. Tel. 17 85 05

Mecodam
Argonautenstraat 98. Tel. 62 03 08

Car Parks (under cover)

Bijenkorf, Beursplein
Europarking, Marnixstraat 250
Krasnapolsky Hotel, St Jansstraat
RAI, Europaboulevard

Chemists (Apotheken)

Times of Opening

8 a.m.–5.30 p.m.

Open at Night

Ring 64 21 11 for information regarding chemists that are open evenings, at night and weekends.

Information Sheet

Chemists provide information sheets listing the chemists supplying an emergency service. When closed, chemists' shops have a notice on the door giving the address of the nearest chemist that is open.

Church Services

Church of England

Christ Church
Groenburgwal 42. Tel. 24 00 77
Services: Sun 9.30 a.m., 10.30 a.m. and 7.30 p.m.

Presbyterian

Church of Scotland
Begijnhof 48. Tel. 24 96 65
Services: daily 10.30 a.m., Wed. 12.40 p.m. and 1.10 p.m., Sun. 9.30 a.m., 10.30 a.m. and 7.30 p.m.

Roman Catholic

Begijnhofkerk
Begijnhof 35. Tel. 22 19 18
Service in English: noon

Cinemas (Bioscoop)

All foreign films are screened in the original version with Dutch sub-titles. Programmes are changed on Thursday; details in the daily papers, also see Programme of Events, p 119.

Cinemas

Alfa 1,2,3,4
Hirschgebouw, Leidseplein
Tel. 27 88 06
Trams 1, 2, 5

Alhambra
Weteringschans 134
Tel. 23 31 92
Trams 1, 2

Bellevue Cinerama
Marnixstraat 400
Tel. 23 48 76
Trams 1, 2, 5

Calypso 1,2
Marnixstraat 402
Tel. 26 62 27
Trams 1, 2, 5

Centraal
Nieuwendijk 67
Tel. 24 89 33
On foot from the Main Station

Cineac
Reguliersbreestraat 31
Tel. 24 36 39
Trams 4, 9, 16, 24, 25

Cinema International 2
Aug. Allebéplein 4
Tel. 15 12 43
Bus 18

Cinecenter Coraline
Pierrot, Peppe Nappa,
Lijnbaansgracht 236
Tel. 23 66 15
Trams 1, 2, 5

City 1,2,3,4,5,6,7
Kleine Gartmanplantsoen, Leidseplein
Tel. 23 45 79
Trams 1, 2, 5

Kriterion, Roeterstraat 170
Tel. 23 17 08
Metro

The Movies, 1,2,3
Haarlemmerdijk 161
Tel. 24 57 90
Buses 18, 22

Parisien
Nieuwendijk 69
Tel. 24 89 33
On foot from Main Station

Rembrandtsplein Theater 1,2
Rembrandtsplein
Tel. 22 35 42
Tram 4

Studio K
Roestersstraat 34
Tel. 23 17 08
Metro

Tuschinski, 1,2,3,4,5,6
Reguliersbreestraat 26
Tel. 26 26 33
Trams 4, 9, 16, 24, 25
Europe's finest old film palace

Consulates

Australia

Australian Consulate
Koninginnegracht 23
The Hague. Tel. (070) 63 09 83
Open: Mon.–Fri. 9 a.m.–1 p.m., 2–5 p.m.

Canada

Canadian Consulate
Sophialaan 7
The Hague. Tel. (070) 61 41 11

South Africa

South African Consulate
Wassenaarseweg 40
The Hague. Tel. (070) 92 45 01

United Kingdom

British Consulate
Koningslaan 44
Tel. 76 43 43
Open: Mon.–Fri. 9.30 a.m.–12.30 p.m., 2.30–4.30 p.m.

United States of America

American Consulate
Museumplein 19
Tel. 79 03 21
Open: Mon.–Fri. 9 a.m.–noon, 2–4 p.m.

Craft Centre (Nederlands Centrum voor Ambachten)

At the Netherlands Craft Centre, near the Main Station, craft workers demonstrate cheese making, glass blowing, clog making, the technique of pewter work, lead glazing, etc. In addition one can see original Delft china painting, pottery making, silver work, spinning and weaving. Articles produced here can be purchased as souvenirs.

Opening times
Feb.–Mar.: Mon., Tues., Thurs.–Sun. 10 a.m.–5 p.m.; Apr.–Oct.: daily 10 a.m.–5 p.m.; Nov.: Mon., Tues., Thurs.–Sun. 10 a.m.–5 p.m.
Closed
Dec. and Jan.

Currency/Currency Regulations

Currency

The unit of currency is the Dutch guilder (hfl) which is made up of 100 cents.

There are banknotes for 5, 10, 25, 50, 100, 250 and 1000 hfl and coins in denominations of 5 (stuiver), 10 (dubbeltje), 25 (kwartje) cents and 1 hfl. (guilder) and 2½ hfl. (rijksdaalder).

Currency Regulations

There are no restrictions on the import or export of Dutch or foreign currency.

Customs Regulations

Visitors to the Netherlands are allowed the usual duty-free allowances of alcohol and tobacco, etc. For goods bought in ordinary shops in Britain or other EEC countries (i.e. duty and tax paid) the allowances are 300 cigarettes or 150 cigarillos or 75 cigars or 400 g of tobacco; 5 litres of still table wine and $1\frac{1}{2}$ litres of alcoholic drinks over 22% vol proof or 3 litres of alcoholic drinks not over 22% vol proof or 3 litres of fortified or sparkling wine, plus 3 litres of still table wine; 75 g of perfume; and 375 cc of toilet-water. For goods bought in a duty-free shop, on a ship or on an aircraft, the allowances are two-thirds of these amounts (250 g of tobacco); the allowances of tobacco goods are doubled for visitors from outside Europe. CB sets operating on 27 MHz may not be imported into the Netherlands.

The duty-free allowances on return to Britain are the same as those for British visitors to the Netherlands.

Duty-free allowances of tobacco and alcoholic drinks apply to persons over 17 years of age.

Department Stores

De Bijenkorf
Damrak 90
Amsterdam's oldest department store, with the broadest range of goods

Vroom & Dreesmann
Kalverstraat (near the mint tower)
Bilderdijkstraat 37–51
Bos en Lommeweg 307–359
Chain department store, not as exclusive as the Bijenkorf

Hema
Nieuwendijk 174
Chain of department stores selling cheap goods; nine branches
Metz & Co.
Keizersgracht 455

Specialist Shops

See Specialist Shops

Diamonds

Amsterdam already had a lively developing diamond trade in the 16th c. and. with the discovery of diamonds in South Africa in 1867, most of which were cut in Amsterdam, this trade expanded and the city became one of the world's most important diamond centres. The supreme skill of Amsterdam's diamond cutters and polishers (see Amsterdam A–Z, Diamond

Gem Diamond Cuts

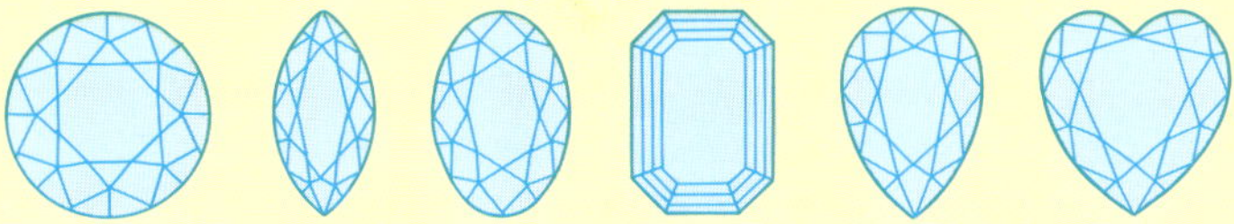

Brilliant **Marquise/Navette** **Oval** **Emerald** **Pear/Drop** **Heart**

cutting) had an important part to play in this. To the connoisseur the phrase "Amsterdam Cut" is synonymous with perfect cutting.

Rough Diamonds

Diamonds (from the Greek word "adamas" meaning invincible) are among the most valuable of precious stones. They are pure carbon crystals, mostly octahedron or dodecahedron, and only rarely cubic, in shape, and extremely hard.

Sources

Diamonds occur in basic and ultrabasic rocks (Kimberlite; workings down to 2000 m (6600 ft) below the ground) and in alluvial deposits. The world's main sources of diamonds are in Africa (Zaire, South Africa, Ghana, Sierra Leone, South West Africa/Namibia, Botswana, Tanzania, Liberia, Central Africa, Ivory Coast, Angola), the USSR (Urals), South America (Venezuela, Brazil, Guyana) and Indonesia and the East Indies.

Uses

More than three-quarters of the diamonds found are used for industrial purposes (drills, stone and glass cutters; drilling, grinding, lapping, polishing; precision instruments, etc.) and barely a quarter are taken for jewellery. Since 1955 it has been possible to manufacture synthetic diamonds for industrial purposes.

Value

The four factors determining the value of a gem diamond, also known as "the four Cs", are its colour, clarity, cut and carat weight.

Cut

The brilliant cut is the best known and most favoured type of cutting and consequently the cut and polished diamonds are usually called brilliants, but strictly speaking this only applies to diamonds where the full cut is in 58 facets. The Marquise (Navette), Oval, Emerald, Drop and Heart cuts also each have 58 facets. Other cuts are the Baguette (simple cut with 24 facets), Octahedron (16 facets) and Carré (a square cut).
Facets are the surfaces created by cutting, which must be arranged at certain angles to each other in order to obtain the optimum refraction of light. The largest horizontal facet is called the "table".

Colour

The colours are known by the following terms:
River – pure-white (blue-white)
Top Wesselton – clear white
Wesselton – white
Top Crystal – slightly tinted white
Crystal – tinted white

Top Cape – considerably tinted white, pale yellowish
Cape (Light Yellow) – yellowish
Diamonds in clear, strong colours such as yellow, brandy-brown, rose, green or blue are the most highly valued.

Clarity

The degree of clarity (recognisable under ×10 magnification):
Internally Flawless, no inclusions
V.V.S.I. – very, very small inclusions
S.I. – small inclusions
I Piqué – visible inclusions
II Piqué – larger inclusions
III Piqué – large inclusions

Carat Weight

The weight of a diamond is measured in carats (1 ct=0·2 g). The word "carat" came originally from Arabic and referred to the dried red-currant seed, used in earlier times for weighing diamonds in India and gold in Africa. The word carat came, via its Dutch use, to enter the language of international trade as a jeweller's measure. Carats, abbreviated as "ct", are used to express the weight of precious stones (1 metric carat=200 mg) and also the purity of gold, i.e. the content of gold in alloys (24 ct=pure gold; 18 ct=750/1000; 14 ct=585/1000 parts of gold).

Famous Diamonds

The largest brilliant is the Cullinan I (530 ct) in the Crown of England; it was part of the largest rough diamond ever found (Cullinan, 3106 ct), which was cut into 105 stones. Other famous large diamonds or brilliants include the Excelsior (rough 955 ct, split up into 22 brilliants, weighing 374 ct altogether); the Jonker (rough 726 ct, split up into 12 brilliants); the Nizzam of Hyderabad (polished 340 ct); the Grand Mogul (polished 280 ct); the Jubilee (rough 651 ct, polished 245 ct); the Star of Yacutia (232 ct); the Orloff (polished 200 ct); the Victoria (rough 469 ct, polished 184 ct); the Koh-i-Nor ("Mountain of Light", rough 191 ct, polished 186 ct); the Regent (rough 410 ct, polished 140 ct); and the Florentine (137 ct).

Diamond Cutting

Guided tours on an individual or group basis:

Amsterdam Diamond Center B.V.
Rokin 1–5. Tel. 24 57 87
Trams 4, 9, 16, 24, 25
Open: Mon.–Wed., Fri., Sat. 10 a.m.–5.30 p.m.; Thurs. 10 a.m.–8.30 p.m., Sun. 11 a.m.–5.30 p.m. from Nov. to Feb.

AS Bonebakker
Rokin 86–90. Tel. 23 22 94
Trams 4, 9, 16, 24, 25
Open: Mon.–Fri. 9.30 a.m.–5.15 p.m.; Sat. 9.30 a.m.–4.45 p.m.; Sun. 10.30 a.m.–4.45 p.m. (Apr. to Sept.)

Coster Diamonds B.V.
Paulus Potterstraat 2–4. Tel. 76 22 22
Trams 1, 2, 5, 16, 24, 25
Opem: Mon.–Sat. 9 a.m.–5 p.m.; Sun. (Apr–Oct.)

Samuel Gassan Diamond House
Nieuwe Achtergracht 17–23. Tel. 22 53 33
Metro
Open: weekdays 9 a.m.–5 p.m.; Sun. 10 a.m.–5 p.m. (Mar.–Oct.)

Holshuysen Stoeltie
Wagenstraat 13–17. Tel. 23 76 01
Trams 4, 9
Open: daily 9 a.m.–5 p.m.

Van Moppes Diamonds
Albert Cuypstraat 2–6. Tel. 76 12 42
Trams 16, 24, 25
Open: daily 8.30 a.m.–5 p.m.

Diamond cutting in Jewellers

See Specialist Shops

Documents

See Travel documents

Doctors

Medical Assistance

Anyone requiring help (doctor, dentist, chemist) should dial either 64 21 11 or 79 18 21. The caller will be given details of the doctor, dentist or chemist available. This service operates day and night.

Out-patient Treatment

Visitors from abroad and members of their families can claim medical attention according to Dutch medical insurance regulations, providing three conditions are fulfilled:
1. The visitor must come from a country with which the Netherlands has an international agreement in this field.
2. Medical attention must be urgently needed and promptly claimed in the manner customary in the Netherlands.
3. An international medical form (or a photocopy) must be given to the doctor, hospital or chemist.

Settlement of Claims

The account is settled directly between the doctor, hospital or chemist and the ANOZ Medical Insurance Bureau. Visitors are therefore advised to have with them a few copies of the international medical insurance form (in Great Britain E.111), to be able to give a copy to the appropriate authority. It will not normally be necessary to settle the account personally.

Invalid Transport ANOZ

Repatriation of a sick person can not be paid for by the ANOZ. The relevant authority for the international agreement in the Netherlands is the ANOZ Medical Insurance Bureau, Box 9069, 3506 GB Utrecht, tel. 030/61 88 81.

Hospitals

See entry

Drugs

All drugs are forbidden by law. Being caught in possession of even less than 30 grams of hashish can attract a fine; with a greater quantity the culprit is likely to be imprisoned. Nevertheless Amsterdam has to contend with 8,000–10,000 heroin addicts. Traffic in drugs has brought with it an increase in crime. The authorities in Amsterdam are making every effort to control the problem of drugs in the city. The notorious Zeedjik district, the centre of the traffic in drugs, has been "cleaned up", thanks to increased daily police patrols. By these measures it is hoped to make it clear to foreign "junkies" (heroin addicts) that their presence is not welcome.

Drug problems

The following organisations give help with drug problems:

JAC

Jongeren Advices Centrum
Amstel 30. Tel. 24 29 49
Open: Mon., Tues., Thurs., Fri. 10 a.m.–noon; Wed., Sat., Sun. 7–10 p.m.
The Jac not only tries to give help in problems with drugs, but also give anonymous and free legal assistance and help with medical and psychiatric problems. It also arranges accommodation.

CAD

Consultatiebureau voor Alcohol en Drugs
Keizersgracht 812. Tel. 23 78 65
Open: Mon.–Fri. 1–3 p.m.

FZA

Federatie van Instellingen voor Alcohol en Drugs
The headquarters can be contacted by telephoning 030/78 07 24, and the caller will be told where the nearest help can be obtained.

Dutch Cuisine

Hotpots

Dutch cuisine is known for its simple, substantial hotpots consisting of potatoes, green vegetables and tasty chunks of meat and crisp-fried bacon. The "Hutspot" is a popular variation made up of equal proportions of potatoes, onions and carrots. Thick green pea soup is a staple national dish in the winter months.

Pancakes

Pancake houses offer an infinite variety of sweet and savoury pancakes (with syrup, apple, liqueur, salami, ham, cheese, mushrooms or bacon). On the "poffertje" stalls hot, fresh small pancakes-cum-doughnuts are fried in cast-iron pans and sold dipped in icing sugar with a knob of butter.

Herring

One of the typical Dutch delicacies is, of course, the herring which can either be bought at the fishmonger's or eaten on the spot, with or without onions, at one of the many herring stalls.

"Broodje half om"

A speciality of the "broodjeswinkels" – which are shops selling fresh bread rolls with a variety of different fillings – is the "broodje half om" which has salted meat on one half and thinly sliced cooked liver on the other. Another speciality is a roll with "tartar" or raw minced beef, and boiled egg. A sweet delicacy is the "Amsterdammetje", a cake stuffed with marzipan.

Sweets

Liquorice fans will be delighted by the many different kinds of "drop", which is Dutch liquorice to suit every taste from sweet to salty. Those who like old-fashioned sweetmeats such as sticks of rock, jelly babies and candy will find plenty to choose from in the sweetshops.

Emergency Phone Numbers (Alarm)

22 22 22 — Police and Ambulance

64 21 11, 79 18 21 — Chemist, Doctor, Dentist

21 21 21 — Fire Brigade

Food and Drink

It is hard to go hungry in Amsterdam. Besides the hearty Dutch cuisine (see entry), the visitor will find an infinite number of speciality restaurants.
If you lack the time or the money to eat in restaurants there is plenty of cheap food to be had; for instance a filled roll from one of the shops called "broodjes" or a snack from the stalls selling fish, etc. on street corners or in the markets (see entry).

Drink

The typical Dutch drinks are beer and genever (gin). An "oude genever" (old gin) is stronger than a "jonge genever" (young gin). The tots of gin (borreltjes) are also served with ice or as long drinks with Coca Cola or tonic water. Imported drinks such as whisky or wine are much more expensive than the local spirits.

Alcohol Tasting Bars

In the "tasting bars", where the principal drinks served are brandy and liqueurs, the glasses are filled so full, that it is necessary to bend down to take the first sip; if the glass is moved the drinker runs the risk of spilling the precious liquid! Every visitor should try this at least once.

Continental Bodega (Sherry Bodega), Lijnbaansgracht 246
De Drie Fleschjes, Gravenstraat 18 (closed Sun.)
Hooghoudt, Reguliersgracht 11 (closed Sun.)
Wijnand Fockink, Pijlsteeg 31 (closed Sun.)

Food Shops

See Specialist shops

Galleries

Amsterdam has approximately 70 galleries and it would be impossible to list them all here. A walk along the canals or through the Jordaan will reveal innumerable small art exhibitions in addition to those listed below.

De Afstap, Oude Leliestraat 12. Tel. 23 14 45
Open: Mon. noon–6 p.m., Tues.–Fri. 10.30 a.m.–6 p.m., Sat. noon–5 p.m.

Amazone, Keizersgracht 678
Open: Tues.–Sat. 10 a.m.–4 p.m., Thurs. also 7–9 p.m., Sun. 1–4 p.m.

Galerie Amsterdam, Warmoesstraat 101. Tel. 24 74 08
Open: Tues.–Fri. noon–6 p.m., Sat. 11 a.m.–5 p.m.
Pictures and drawings of Amsterdam

Artigalerie, Spui 1a. Tel. 23 33 67
Open: Tues.–Sat. noon–6 p.m.

Elisabeth den Bieman de Haas, Nieuwe Spiegelstraat 44. Tel. 26 10 12
Open: Tues.–Sat. 11 a.m.–5 p.m.
Modern drawings

Galerie Chieron, P.C. Hooftstraat 153. Tel. 64 58 13
Open: Tues.–Sat. 10.30 a.m.–4 p.m.

Maison Descartes, Vijzelgracht 2a
Open: Mon.–Fri. 10 a.m.–6 p.m.
Photographic gallery

Galerie Drie 05, Overtoom 305. Tel. 16 54 27
Open: Tues.–Sat. noon–6 p.m.

Galerie d'Eendt, Spui 272
Open: Tues.–Sat. 10 a.m.–6 p.m.

Galerie Forum, Herengracht 156. Tel. 26 52 07
Open: Tues.–Fri. noon–5.30 p.m., Sat. noon–4 p.m.

Galerie Hamer, Leliegracht 38. Tel. 26 73 94
Open: Tues.–Sat. 1–5.30 p.m.
International naïve art

Hologram Gallery, Leidsestraat 30. Tel. 22 97 49
Open: Mon.–Sat. noon–6 p.m., Sun. 1–6 p.m.

Galerie Imago, N.Z. Voorburgwal 371. Tel. 27 70 46
Open: Wed.–Sat. noon–5.30 p.m.

Atelier 408, Herengracht 408
Open: Wed.–Sat. noon–5.30 p.m.

Gallery Jeroen Bechtold, Korte Leidsedwarsstraat 159. Tel. 24 98 71
Open: Thurs., Fri., Sat. 11 a.m.–5 p.m.
Permanent exhibitions of modern studio porcelain from the Netherlands

Galerie K318, Keizersgracht 318. Tel. 25 70 04
Open: Wed.–Sat. 1–5 p.m.

Galerie Lemaire, Reguliersgracht 80. Tel. 23 70 27
Open: Mon.–Fri. 10 a.m.–5.30 p.m., Sat. 11 a.m.–2 p.m.
Permanent exhibitions of ethnographic objects and exotic textile work

Lieve Hemel Galerie, Vijzelgracht 6–8. Tel. 23 00 60
Open: Tues.–Sat. noon–6 p.m.
Netherlands artists of "New Realism"

Galerie Mokum, O.Z. Voorburgwal 334. Tel. 24 39 58
Open: Mon.–Sat. 11 a.m.–5 p.m.
Netherlands artists of "New Realism"

Prentengalerie, Kerkstraat 301. Tel. 25 22 89
Open: Tues.–Sat. 11 a.m.–6 p.m.

Galerie Siau, Keizersgracht 267. Tel. 26 72 21
Open: Tues.–Sat. 11 a.m.–6 p.m., Sun. 2–5 p.m.

Galerie Steltman, Westermarkt 27
Open: Tues.–Sat. 11 a.m.–6 p.m.

STOV, L. Leidsedwarsstraat 208. Tel. 23 09 67
Open: Tues.–Fri. 10.30 a.m.–5.30 p.m., Sat. 11 a.m.–4 p.m.

Galerie de Witte Voet, Kerkstraat 149. Tel. 25 84 12
Open: Tues.–Sat. noon–5 p.m.

Handicapped Visitors

A special brochure for handicapped visitors to the Netherlands can be obtained from the Dutch Tourist Offices (see Information)

Hospitals

Ambulance

Call 5 55 55 55

Casualty Services

Hospitals providing a 24-hour casualty service:

Academisch Medisch Centrum, Meibergdreef 9. Tel. 5 66 91 11

V.U. Ziekenhuis, de Boelelaan 1117. Tel. 5 48 91 11

Lucas Ziekenhuis, Jan Tooropstraat 164. Tel. 5 10 89 11

Onze Lieve Vrouwe Gasthuis, 1e Oosterparkstraat 179.
Tel. 5 99 91 11

Slotervaartziekenhuis, Louwesweg 6. Tel. 5 12 93 33

Ziekenhuis Amsterdam-Noord, Distelkade 21. Tel. 36 89 22

Stichting Kruispost, O.Z. Voorburgwal 129. Tel. 24 90 31

Emergency Service

The emergency number is 64 21 11, 79 18 21

Hotels

Reservations

The VVV (tourist information centre) can help with finding a suitable hotel, but visitors must call at the office personally. The VVV also supplies a free hotel guide (see Information).

Tourists planning to visit Amsterdam during public holidays such as Easter or Whitsun should book accommodation in good time. Either direct with the hotel or through the National Reserverings Centrum (NRC), Box 404 AK 2260 Leidschendam, Tel. 070/20 25 00. Exact dates, hotel category and type or room required should be given.

	Single	Double
*****	300–400	370–470
****	200–300	220–360
***	100–175	120–210
**	75–120	100–130
*	40–90	60–110

Luxury Hotels
*****

Amstel, Prof. Tulpplein 1. Tel. 22 60 60
Amsterdam Apollo, Apollolaan 2. Tel. 73 59 22
Amsterdam Hilton, Apollolaan 138–140. Tel. 78 07 80
Amsterdam Marriott, Stadhouderskade 21. Tel. 83 51 51
Amsterdam Sonesta, Kattengat 1. Tel. 21 22 23
De L'Europe, Nieuwe Doelenstraat 2–4. Tel. 2–4. Tel. 23 48 36
Golden Tulip Hotel Barbizon, Stadhouderskade 7. Tel. 85 13 51
Okura Amsterdam, Ferd, Bolstraat 157. Tel. 78 71 11

First Class Hotels
****

Acca, Van de Veldestraat 3a. Tel. 62 52 62
Alexander, Prinsengracht 444, Tel. 26 77 21
American, Leidsekade 97. Tel. 24 53 22
Amsterdam Ascot, Damrak 95–98
Crest Hotel Amsterdam, De Boelelaan 2. Tel. 46 23 00
Doelen Crest, Nieuwe Doelenstraat 24, Tel. 22 07 22
Etap Hotel Capitool, N.Z. Voorburgwal 67. Tel. 27 59 00
Garden, Dijsselhofphantsoen 7. Tel. 64 21 21
Grand Hotel Krasnapolsky, Dam 9. Tel. 5 54 60 48
(facilities for wheelchairs)
Novotel Amsterdam, Europaboulevard 10. Tel. 5 41 11 23
Die Port van Cleve, N.Z. Voorburgwal 178–180. Tel. 22 64 29
Pulitzer, Prinsengracht 315–331. Tel. 22 83 33
Schiller Crest, Rembrandtplein 22–36. Tel. 23 16 60

Very Comfortable Hotels
***

AMS Hotel Beethoven, Beethovenstraat 43. Tel. 64 48 16
AMS Hotel Terdam, Tesselchadestraat 23. Tel. 12 68 76
Apollofirst, Apollolaan 123. Tel. 73 03 33
Arthur Frommer, Noorderstraat 46. Tel. 22 03 28
Atlas, Van Eeghenstraat 64. Tel. 76 63 36
Carlton Crest, Vijzelstraat 2–18. Tel. 22 22 66
Damrak, Damrak 49. Tel. 26 24 98
Delphi, Apollolaan 101–105. Tel. 79 51 52
Golden Tulip Centraal, Stadhouderskade 7. Tel. 18 57 65
Jan Luyken, Jan Luykenstraat 58. Tel. 76 41 11
Memphis, De Lairessestraat 87. Tel. 73 31 41
Owl, Roemer Visscherstraat 1. Tel. 18 94 84
Westropa II, Nassaukade 389–390. Tel. 83 49 35
Zandbergen, Willemsparkweg 205. Tel. 76 93 21

Comfortable Hotels
**

Aalborg, Sarphatipark, 106–108. Tel. 79 90 57
Aalders, Jan Luykenstraat 13–15. Tel. 73 40 27
Ambassade, Herengracht 341. Tel. 26 23 33
AMS Hotel Holland, P.C. Hooftstraat 162. Tel. 76 42 53
Asterisk, Den Texstraat 14–16. Tel. 26 23 96
Atlanta, Rembrandtplein 8–10. Tel. 25 35 85
Belfort, Surinameplein 53. Tel. 17 43 33
Borgmann, Koningslaan 48. Tel. 73 52 52
Canal House, Keizersgracht 148. Tel. 22 51 82

Casa 400, James Watstraat 75. Tel. 65 11 71
Casa Cara, Emmastraat 24. Tel. 62 31 35
Centralpark "West", Roemer Visscherstraat 27. Tel. 85 22 85
Cordial, Rokin 62–64. Tel. 26 44 11
Cynthia, Vondelstraat 44–46. Tel. 18 24 28
Eden, Amstel 144. Tel. 26 62 43
Engeland, Roemer Visscherstraat 30. Tel. 18 08 62
Euromotel E–9, Joan Muyskenweg 10. Tel. 65 81 81
Eureka, 's–Gravelandseveer 3–4. Tel. 26 70 72
Fantasia, Nieuwe Keizersgracht 16. Tel. 24 88 58
De Gerstekorrel, Damstraat 22–24. Tel. 24 13 67
De Gouden Kettingh, Keizersgracht 268. Tel. 24 82 87
Heemskerk, J.W. Brouwersstraat 25. Tel. 79 49 80
Hestia, Roemer Visscherstraat 7. Tle. 10 08 01
Hoksbergen, Singel 301. Tel. 26 60 43
Imperial, Thorbeckeplein 9. Tel. 22 00 51
De Koreaner, Damrak 50. Tel. 22 08 55
De Lantaerne, Leidsegracht 111. Tel. 23 22 21
Marianne, Nicolaas Maesstraat 107. Tel. 79 79 72
Mikado, Amstel 107–111. Tel. 23 70 68
Museum, P.C. Hooftstraat 2. Tel. 62 14 02
Nicolaas Witsen, Nicolaas Witsenstraat 4. Tel. 23 61 43
Nova, N.Z. Voorburgwal 276–280. Tel. 23 00 66
Omega, Jacob Obrechtstraat 31. Tel. 64 51 82
Parklane, Plantage Parklaan 16. Tel. 22 48 04
Parkzicht, Roemer Visscherstraat 33. Tel. 18 19 54
Piet Hein, Vossiusstraat 53. Tel. 62 72 05
Prins Hendrik, Prins Hendrikkade 52. Tel. 23 79 69
Prinsen, Vondelstraat 36–38. Tel. 16 23 23
Rokin, Rokin 73. Tel. 26 74 56
De Roode Leeuw, Damrak 93–94. Tel. 24 03 96
Sander, Jacob Obrechtstraat 69. Tel. 62 24 95
Sipermann, Roemer Visscherstraat 35. Tel. 16 18 66
Slotania, Slotermeerlaan 133. Tel. 13 45 68
Smit, P.C. Hooftstraat 24–26. Tel. 76 63 43
Terminus, Beursstraat 11–19. Tel. 23 30 25
Toren, Keizersgracht 164. Tel. 22 60 33
Toren Star, Keizersgracht 146. Tel. 22 22 04
Trianon, J.W. Brouwersstraat 3. Tel. 73 20 73
Vondel, Vondelstraat 28–30. Tel. 12 01 20
Vondelhof, Vondelstraat 24, Tel. 12 01 20
Westropa I, 1e Const. Huygensstraat 103–105. Tel. 18 88 08
Wiechmann, Prinsengracht 328–330. Tel. 26 33 21
Wilhelmina, Koninginneweg 169. Tel. 62 54 67

Modest Hotels
*

Abba. Overtoom 122. Tel. 18 30 58
Van Acker, J.W. Brouwersstraat 14. Tel. 79 80 76
Acro, Jan Luykenstraat 4244. Tel. 62 05 26
Albatros, Nieuwendijk 100. Tel. 25 90 76
Amstelbrug, Weesperzijde 28. Tel. 94 64 07
Armada, Keizersgracht 713–715. Tel. 23 29 80
Arsenal, Frans van Mierisstraat 97. Tel. 79 22 09
Belga, Hartenstraat 8. Tel. 24 90 80
De Bijenkorf, Prins Hendrikkade 37–38. Tel. 24 28 17
City Hotel Amsterdam, Prins Hendrikkade 130. Tel. 23 08 36
Digla, Keizersgracht 37–39. Tel. 24 96 00
Fita, Jan Luykenstraat 37. Tel. 79 09 76
Flipper, Borssenburgstraat 5. Tel. 76 19 32
Van Haalen, Prinsengracht 520. Tel. 26 43 34
Harten Vijf, Hartenstraat 5. Tel. 24 57 17

De La Haye, Leidsegracht 114. Tel. 24 40 44
Hegra, Herengracht 269. Tel. 23 53 48
Hemony, Hemonystraat 7. Tel. 71 42 41
Holbein, Holbeinstraat 5. Tel. 62 88 32
Impala, Leidsekade 77. Tel. 23 47 06
Jupiter, 2e Helmersstraat 14. Tel. 18 71 32
Kap, Den Texstraat 5b. Tel. 24 59 08
Van de Kasteelen, Frans van Meirisstraat 34. Tel. 79 89 95
King, Leidsekade 85–86. Tel. 24 96 03
De Leydsche Hof, Leidsegracht 14. Tel. 23 21 48
Linda, Stradhouderskade 131, Tel. 62 56 68
Maas, Leidsekade 91. Tel. 23 38 68
Middelberg, Koninginneweg 149. Tel. 76 53 92
De Munck, Achtergracht 3. Tel. 23 62 83
Museumzicht, Jan Luykenstraat 22. Tel. 71 29 54
Olzewski, Plantage Muidergracht 89. Tel. 23 62 41
Oosterpark, Oosterpark 72. Tel. 93 00 49
Van Ostade, Van Ostadestraat 123, Tel. 79 34 52
P.C. Hooft, P.C. Hooftstraat 63. Tel. 62 71 07
Prinsenhof, Prinsengracht 810. Tel. 23 17 72
Van Rooyen 2e Helmersstraat 6. Tel. 18 45 77
Schirmann, Prins Hendrikkade 23. Tel. 24 19 42
Seven Bridges, Reguliersgracht 31. Tel. 23 13 29
Sphinx, Weteringschans 82. Tel. 27 36 80
Tabu, Marnixstraat 386. Tel. 22 75 11
Titus, Leidsekade 74, Tel. 26 57 58
Victorie, Victorieplein 42, Tel. 73 39 88
Vincent van Gogh, Van de Veldestraat 5. Tel. 79 60 02
Vullings, P.C. Hooftstraat 78. Tel. 71 21 09
Het Wapen van Amsterdam, Damrak 58. Tel. 24 92 63
Washington, Frans de Mierisstraat 10. Tel. 79 67 54
Weber, Marnixstraat 397, Tel. 27 05 74
Von Wehde, Korte van Eeghenstraat 8. Tel. 76 21 31
Westertoren, Raadhuisstraat 35b. Tel. 24 46 39
De Wilde, Koninginneweg 93. Tel. 62 78 94
Winston, Warmoesstraat 129. Tel. 23 13 80
Wijnnobel, Vossiusstraat 9. Tel. 62 22 98

Inexpensive Accommodation for Young People

There are many inexpensive hotels and other accommodation in Amsterdam which are especially suitable for younger visitors.

Youth Hotels

Jeugdhotel Adam en Eva
Sarphatisstraat 105. Tel. 24 62 06
Open: mid Mar.–end of Dec.
108 beds in rooms containing from one to eight beds. Rooms with several beds are not segregated according to sex.

Studentenhotel Adolesce
Niuwe Keizerdgracht 26. Tel. 26 39 59
Open throughout the year
120 beds, 11 dormitories, 9 bedrooms

Acro Low Budget
Jan Luykenstraat 42–44. Tel. 62 05 26
Open throughout the year
144 beds. 1 dormitory, 20 bedrooms

Bob's Youth Hotel
N.Z. Voorabrgwal 92. Tel. 23 00 63
Open throughout the year
160 beds, 15 dormitories, 5 bedrooms

Cok Studentenhotel, Koninginneweg 34. Tel. 64 61 11
Open throughout the year
210 beds, 140 rooms (single, double and rooms with several beds)

Jeugdhotel Eben Haezer
Bloemstraat 179. Tel. 24 47 17
Open throughout the year
114 beds, 5 dormitories

Hans Brinker Stutel
Kerkstraat 136–138. Tel. 22 06 88
Open throughout the year
275 beds, 18 dormitories, 54 bedrooms

Jeugdhotel Kabul
Warmoesstraat 42. Tel. 23 71 58
Open throughout the year
262 beds, 17 dormitories, 33 bedrooms

Jeugdhotel The Shelter
Barndesteeg 21–25. Tel. 25 32 30
Open throughout the year, except for the last two weeks in January
168 beds, 8 bedrooms

Sleep-in Mauritskade
's-Gravezandestraat 1. Tel. 94 74 44
Open: beginning of Jun.–mid Sept. and at Easter and Whitsun.
Accommodation for 750, 8 bedrooms

International Student Centre
Keizersgracht 15. Tel. 25 13 64
Open throughout the year
120 beds

Travel
Beursstraat 23. Tel. 26 65 32
61 beds

Further information about youth hotels and all kinds of accommodation can be obtained from the VVV Tourist Bureau (see Information)

'Umbrella' Organisation

Stichting Nederlandse Jeugdherberg Centrale (NJHC), Prof. Tulpplein 4. Tel. 26 44 33
1018 GX Amsterdam
This organisation runs more than 50 youth hostels in the Netherlands which are not exclusively for members of a youth-hostel organisation or holders of an international youth-hostel card.

Tariff (1986)

Bed and breakfast: 16 hfl.
Packed lunch: from 5 hfl.
Hot meal: from 11.00 hfl.
Prices depend on the category of the accommodation.
Sleeping Bag, etc: 4.5 hfl.
In many youth hostels a kitchen is available for preparation of meals.

Youth Hostels

Stadsdoelen
Kloveniersburgwal 97. Tel. 24 68 32
Open: mid Mar.–mid Oct.
184 beds, 9 dormitories, kitchen available for personal use.

Vondelpark
Zandpad 5. Tel. 83 17 44
Open throughout the year
316 beds, 35 dormitories; kitchen available for personal use.

Information

Netherlands National Tourist Office

Australia

Suite 302, 5 Elizabeth Street
Sydney N.S.W. 2000. Tel. 02–276921

Canada

One Dundas Street West, P.O. Box 19
Suite 2108, Toronto, Ontario M5G 1Z3
Tel. 0 (416) 598–2830/2831

850 Hastings Street, Suite 214
Vancouver, B.S. V6C 1E1
Tel. 0 (604) 684–5720. Telex 04–55133

South Africa

Union Square (2nd Floor)
Cnr. Plein and Klein Street, P.O. Box 8624
Johannesburg. Tel. 011–236991

United Kingdom

25–28 Buckingham Gate,
London SW1E 6LD
Tel. 01–630 0451. Telex 269005

United States of America

576 Fifth Avenue, New York N.Y. 10036
Tel. 0 (212) 245–5320. Telex 620081

681 Market Street, Room 941
San Francisco, Cal. 94105
Tel. 0 (415) 781–3387

Amsterdam

Tourist Information Centre (VVV)
Stationsplein 10.
Tel. 26 64 44 (Mon.–Sat. 9 a.m.–5.30 p.m.)
Open: Easter–30 Sept.: Mon.–Sat. 9 a.m.–midnight; Sun. 9 a.m.–9 p.m.; 1 Oct.–Easter: Mon.–Sat. 9 a.m.–7 p.m., Sun. 10 a.m.–1.30 p.m., 2.30–5 p.m.

VVV is the most important source of information for tourists: hotel booking (for all the Netherlands), room reservations (for Amsterdam), advance booking for theatres and concerts, as well as information about all cultural events, booking of excursions, special information for young people, public transport details, car hire, etc.

VVV Leidsestraat 106
Open: Easter–30 Sept.: daily 9 a.m.–10.30 p.m.; 1 Oct–Easter: Mon.–Fri. 10.30 a.m.–7 p.m., Sat. 10.30 a.m.–9 p.m., Sun. 10.30 a.m.–6 p.m.
Trams: 1, 2, 5

VVV Utrechtsweg A2 (opposite Euromotel)
Open: Easter–30 Sept.: Mon.–Sat. 10.30 a.m.–2 p.m., 2.30–6.30 p.m.
Tram: 25

In Aalsmeer

VVV Aalsmeer
Stationsweg 8. Tel. 02977/2 53 74
Open: Easter–30 Sept.: Mon.–Fri. 9 a.m.–5 p.m., Sat. 10 a.m.–noon

In Alkmaar

VVV Alkmaar
Waagplein 3. Tel. 072/11 42 84
Open: In the season – Mon.–Fri. 9 a.m.–5 p.m., Sat. 10 a.m.–noon

In Delft

VVV Delft
Markt 85. Tel. 015/12 61 00
Open: In the season – Mon.–Fri. 9 a.m.–5 p.m., Sat. 10 a.m.–noon

In Edam

VVV Edam
Kleine Kerkstraat 17. Tel. 02993/7 17 27
Open: Apr.–Sept.: Mon.–Fri. 10 a.m.–12.30 p.m., 1.30–5 p.m., Sat. noon–5 p.m.; Oct.–Mar.: Mon.–Sat. 10.30–noon

In Hoorn

VVV Hoorn
"Statenpoort"
Nieuwstraat 23. Tel. 02290/11 83 42
Open: In the season – Mon.–Fri. 9 a.m.–5 p.m., Sat. 9 a.m.–noon

In Leiden

VVV Leiden
Stationsplein 210. Tel. 071/14 68 46
Open: In the season – Mon.–Fri. 9 a.m.–5 p.m., Sat. 10 a.m.–noon

In Monnickendam/Marken

VVV Monnickendam
Zarken 2. Tel. 02995/19 98
Open: Apr.–Sept.: Mon.–Sat. 10 a.m.–7 p.m.; Oct.–Mar. Mon.–Sat. 10 a.m.–12.30 p.m.

In Oudewater

VVV Oudewater
IJsselveere 17. Tel. 03486/14 53
Open: In the season – Mon.–Fri. 9 a.m.–5 p.m., Sat. 10 a.m.–noon

In Volendam

VVV Volendam
Zeestraat 21. Tel. 02993/6 37 47
Open: Apr.–Sept.: Mon.–Fri. 9 a.m.–5 p.m., Sat. and Sun. 10 a.m.–5 p.m.

In Zaandam

VVV Zaandam
Gedempte Gracht 76. Tel. 075/16 22 21
Open: In the season – Mon.–Fri. 9 a.m.–5.30 p.m., Sat. 10 a.m.–1 p.m.

In De Rijp

VVV De Rijp-Graft
Jan Boonplein 8. Tel. 02997/16 51
Open: In the season – Mon.–Fri. 9 a.m.–5 p.m., Sat. 10 a.m.–noon

Practical Information

In Purmerend

VVV Purmerend
Kaasemarkt 3. Tel. 02990/5 25 25
Open: In the season – Mon.–Fri. 9 a.m.–5 p.m., Sat. 10 a.m.–4 p.m.

In Zandvoort

VVV Zandvoort
Schoolplein 1. Tel. 02507/1 79 47
Open: In the season – Mon.–Fri. 9 a.m.–5 p.m., Sat. 10 a.m.–noon

Jazz

See Cafés

Libraries (Bibliotheek)

Bibliothek Gemeentearchiev (local archives)
Amsteldijk 67. Tel. 64 69 16
Trams: 3, 4
Open: Mon.–Fri. 8.45 a.m.–4.45 p.m.

Historische Verzameling van de Universiteit van Amsterdam (historical collection)
O.Z. Voorburgwal 231. Tel. 5 25 33 39
Near the Centraal Station
Open: Mon.–Fri. 9 a.m.–5 p.m.

Bibliothek Joods Historisch Museum
The Jewish Museum moves to a new home in 1987, therefore the museum and library are closed from 3 Nov. 1986–2 May 1987. The new address can be obtained from the VVV (see Practical Information, Information)

Bibliothek Multatuli Museum
Korsjepoortsteeg 20. Tel. 24 74 27
Trams: 1, 2, 5, 13, 17
Open: Tues. 10 a.m.–5 p.m. by arrangement
Works by the writer Multatuli

Bibliothek Nederlands Filmmuseum
Vondelpark 3. Tel. 83 16 46
Trams: 1, 2, 3, 5, 6, 12
Open: Tues.–Thurs. 9 a.m.–5 p.m.

Bibliothek Nederlands Theater Instituut
Herengracht 166. Tel. 23 51 04
Trams: 13, 14, 17
Open: Tues.–Fri. 11 a.m.–5 p.m.

Bibliothek Nederlands Scheepvaart Museum (marine museum)
Kattenburgerplain 1. Tel. 26 22 55
Bus: 22, 28
Open: only by written or telephone arangement

Bibliothek Rijksmuseum
See A–Z, Rijksmuseum

Bibliothek Schriftmuseum (Amsterdam University)
Singel 425. Tel. 5 25 24 76
Trams: 1, 2, 4, 5, 9, 16, 24, 25
Open: Mon.–Fri. 10 a.m.–1 p.m., 2–4.30 p.m.

Bibliothek Stedelijk Museum
See A–Z, Stedelijk Museum

Bibliothek Tropenmuseum
Linnaeusstraat 2. Tel. 5 68 82 00
Trams: 3, 6, 9, 10
Open: Tues.–Fri. 10 a.m.–4.30 p.m., Sun. noon–4.30 p.m.

Bibliothek Universiteit van Amsterdam
Singel 425
Trams: 1, 2, 4, 5, 9, 13, 14, 16, 17, 24, 25; Metro
Open: 11 a.m.–5 p.m.

Bibliothek Van Gogh Museum
See A–Z, Van Gogh Museum

Zoologisch Museum
Plantage Middenlaan 53. Tel. 5 22 32 98
Trams: 6, 7, 9, 10, 14
Open: Tues.–Fri. 9.30 a.m.–4.30 p.m.

Lost Property (Buro gevonden voorwerpen)

General

Elandsgracht 117 (police station). Tel. 5 59 91 11
Open: Mon. 1–4 p.m., Tues.–Fri. 11 a.m.–4 p.m.

Bicycles

Mastenbroek, Leidsegracht 76. Tel. 23 23 12

Markets

Antiques

See Antiques

Birds

By the Noorderkerk
Open: Saturday mornings

Books

Oudemanhuispoort
See Amsterdam A–Z, Oudemanhuispoort

Fabrics

Noordermarkt
by the Noorderkerk (Jordaan)
Open: Monday mornings
For "lapjes" (fabric and remnants) and secondhand clothing

Flea Market

Waterlooplein
See Amsterdam A–Z, Vlooienmarkt

Flowers

On the Singel
Trams: 1, 2, 4, 5, 9, 16, 24, 25
Open: Mon.–Sat. 9 a.m.–5 p.m.
Cut flowers and pot plants in all sizes, colours and shapes

Amstelveld
Open: Monday mornings, May–October
Plants and herbs for gardens and balconies, house plants

Food, Clothing and Textiles

Albert Cuypmarkt
See Amsterdam A–Z, Albert Cuypmarkt

Dappermarkt (behind the Tropical Museum – see entry)
Open: Tues.–Sat.

Ten-Katemarkt (near the Kinkerstraat)
Open: daily

Stamps

N.Z. Voorburgwal (opposite No. 280)
Trams: 1, 2, 5
Open: Wed., Sat. from 1 p.m.

Museums

Allard-Pierson-Museum
Oude Turfmarkt 127
Trams: 4, 9, 14, 16, 24, 25
Open: Tues.–Fri. 10 a.m.–5 p.m., Sat. and Sun. and public holidays 1–5 p.m.
Closed: Mon., 1 Jan., 5 May
Admission fee

The archaeological collection of Amsterdam University – one of the biggest of its kind in the world.
Large collection of Greek and Roman antiquities, as well as ancient Egyptian mummies, figures of gods and animals, and sarcophagi. In addition there are collections from the Near East, Mesopotamia, Iran, Cyprus, the Cyclades and from Mycenae.

Museum Amstelkring
See Amsterdam A–Z, Museum Amstelkring

Amsterdamse Bos (Arboretum)
See Amsterdam A–Z, Amsterdamse Bos

Anne Frank Huis
See Amsterdam A–Z, Anne Frank Huis

Aviodome (National Aeronautics and Space Travel Museum)
See Amsterdam A–Z, Schiphol Airport

Open: Apr.–Oct.: Mon.–Sat. 10 a.m.–5 p.m., Nov.–Mar.: Thurs.–Sun. 10 a.m.–5 p.m.
Closed: Mon., 26, 31 Dec., 1 Jan.
Admission fee

Exhibition showing the history of aviation in the Aviodome, with 20 veteran aeroplanes, models of satellites and reconstructions of famous aircraft and flying machines as well as film shows and demonstrations

Banketbakkersmuseum or Culinair Historisch Museum
Wibaustraat 220–222
Open: Wed. 10 a.m.–4 p.m., closed during school holidays

Museums (cont.)

The history of pastrymaking in a former bakery, with tools of the baker's trade and other curios

Bijbels Museum (Bible museum)
Herengracht 366
Trams: 1, 2, 5
Open: Tues.–Sat. 10 a.m.–5 p.m.; Sun. and public holidays 1–5 p.m.
Closed: 1 Jan., 5 May
Admission fee
A collection of biblical archaeology in two beautiful old houses (18th c.) on one of the canals, including finds from Egypt and Palestine, priceless antique bibles and sacred Jewish artefacts
Regular special exhibitions

Bilderdijkmuseum
de Boelelaan 1105, in main building of the Free University.
Tel. 45 43 68
Buses: 23, 65, CN 173
Open: By prior arrangement (by letter or telephone) only
A collection on the site of the Free University of books and curios from the life of the Dutch poet Willem Bilderdijk (1756–1831), known for his translations of the classics and patriotic poems and plays
Admission fee

Frederik van Eeden Museum
Singel 425
(University Library)
Open: Mon.–Fri. 10 a.m.–1 p.m. and 2–4.30 p.m.
Guided tours by arrangement
Trams: 1, 2, 4, 5, 9, 16, 24, 25
A museum devoted to the Dutch writer and social reformer Fredrik van Eeden (1860–1932) who founded a short-lived community in 1898 based on his socio-romantic beliefs

Electrische Museum Tramlijn
Haarlemmermeerstation, Amstelveenseweg 264
Trams: 6, 16; Buses: 15, 23, 60 CN 170, 171, 172, 125, 146, 147
Open: 30, Mar.–25 Oct.: Sun. and public holidays 10 a.m.–6 p.m.; 5 July–6 Sept. Sat. noon–6 p.m.; admission fee
Trips on old trams from Haarlemmermeer Station from where, until 1950, the steam train to Amstelveen, Aalsmeer and Uithoorn departed. The old rails were suitable for trams, and today the museum railway takes visitors through the Amsterdamse Bos and as far as Amstelveen, a stretch of about 6 km/4 miles. Of a total of 60 trams, which were built between 1910 and 1950 not only in the Netherlands but also in Germany and Austria, 15 are regularly used. This is a wonderful trip, especially for children

Filmmuseum
Vondelpark 3
Trams: 1, 2, 5
Open: Tues.–Fri. 10 a.m.–5 p.m.
Closed: Mon. and public holidays
Admission fee
This museum, housed in a pavilion in the park, uses models to tell the story of film-making and mounts special exhibitions,

Museums (cont.)

with exhibits from foreign film museums. Film buffs can enjoy screenings of films by particular directors, etc. Plus a large reference library

Museum Fodor
Keizersgracht 609
Trams: 4, 16, 24, 25
Open: daily 11 a.m.–5 p.m.
Admission fee
Exhibition of works by contemporary artists, especially those living in Amsterdam
The museum, first opened in 1863, originally contained the collection of the coalmerchant C. J. Fodor which is today in the Amsterdam History Museum (see Amsterdam A–Z, Amsterdams Historisch Museum)

Geologisch Museum UvA (Universiteit van Amsterdam)
Nieuwe Prinsengracht 130
Tram: 9; Metro
Open: Mon.–Fri. 9 a.m.–5 pm.
Closed: public holidays, when these fall on Mon.–Fri.
Admission fee
Collection of stones, fossils, minerals, etc.

Historische Verzameling van de Universiteit van Amsterdam
Oude Zijds Voorburgwal 231 not for from Centraal Station
Open: Mon.–Fri. 9 a.m.–5 p.m.
Admission fee
A collection of posters, books, documents, paintings, etc. illustrating the history of the university since 1632. The Agnetien Chapel, in which it is housed, has been part of the university since 1470 and was restored in 1921

Historisch Museum
See Amsterdam A–Z, Amsterdams Historisch Museum

Museum Willet Holthuysen
Herengracht 605
Trams: 4, 9
Open: Tues.–Sat. 10 a.m.–5 p.m.; Sun. and public holidays 1–5 p.m.
A typical 17th c. patrician house, which has been made into a museum, on the Keizersgracht (see Amsterdam A–Z, Keizersgracht) with an 18th c. garden

Informatie-Centrum Dienst Ruimtelijke Ordening (Information centre of environmental planning)
Keizersgracht 440
Trams: 1, 2, 5, 7, 10
Open: Tues.–Fri. 12.30–4.30 p.m.; Thurs. also 6–9 p.m.
Exhibition illustrating the municipal building programme of Amsterdam. A permanent exhibition shows the historical environmental development of the city. The renovation of the city is comprehensively demonstrated by means of illustrations, drawings, slides and town plans

Nederlands Instituut voor Nijverheid en Techniek (NINT) (Dutch Institute for industry and technology)
Tolstraat 129
Open: Mon.–Fri. 10 a.m.–4 p.m., Sat., Sun. and public holidays 1–5 p.m.
Admission fee

Museums (cont.)

Joods Historisch Museum (history of Amsterdam's Jewish population)
See Amsterdam A–Z, Waaggebouw

Werft 'T Kromhout (Wharf museum)
Hoogte Kadijk 147
Bus: 22
Open: Mon.–Sat. 10 a.m.–4 p.m., Sun. 1–4 p.m.; closed public holidays
Admission fee
Permanent exhibition of marine engines, models and shipbuilding tools. There are some older small vessels afloat

Museum van Loon
Keizersgracht 672
Trams: 16, 24, 25
Open: Mon. 10 a.m.–noon, 1–5 p.m.
Admission fee
This canal-house museum, dating from 1672, has been furnished in the patrician style typical of 1750 and besides various kinds of objets d'art houses a collection of over 50 17th and 18th c. family portraits. It stands in a beautifully landscaped Rococo garden

Madame Tussaud in Amsterdam
Kalverstraat 156
Trams: 1, 2, 5, 9, 16, 24, 25
Open: daily 10 a.m.–6 p.m.
Closed: 25 Dec.
Admission fee
The only "Madam Tussaud" outside London. As well as contemporary personalities – Queen Beatrix, Margaret Thatcher, François Mitterand – visitors can also meet Napoleon and Tsar Peter the Great. A whole room is devoted to Rembrandt, Hieronymus Bosch is represented by his "Garden of Desires" and in a kaleidoscope can be seen notable pop stars. The workshop, where the wax models are produced, can also be visited

Multatuli Museum
Korsjespoortsteeg 20. Tel. 24 74 27
Trams: 1, 2, 5, 13, 17
Buses: 21, CN/GVB 67, CN 143, 144, 145, 170, 171, 172
Open: Tues. 10 a.m.–5 p.m. by appointment
Exhibition commemorating the Dutch writer Multatuli, whose real name was Eduard Douwes Dekker (1820–1887), and who, in his free-thinking, humanitarian novels (including "Max Havelaar or The Dutch on Java"), sharply attacked the Dutch colonial system

Nederlands Persmuseum (Museum of the Press)
University Library, Singel 425
Trams: 1, 2, 4, 5, 9, 13, 14, 16, 17, 24, 25; Metro
Open: Mon.–Fri. 11 a.m.–5 p.m.
A collection of newspapers, magazines, posters, pamphlets and cartoons since the early 17th c.
Temporary exhibitions

Rembrandthuis
See Amsterdam A–Z, Rembrandthuis

Museums (cont.)

Rijksmuseum
See Amsterdam A–Z, Rijksmuseum

Rijksmuseum Vincent van Gogh
See Amsterdam A–Z, van Gogh Museum

Scheepvaartmuseum (Maritime Museum)
Kattenburgerplein 1
Buses: 22, 28
Open: Tues.–Sat. 10 a.m.–5 p.m.; Sun. and public holidays 1–5 p.m.
Closed: Mon., 1 Jan.
Admission fee
Collection of model ships, globes, navigational instruments and maritime pictures

Schriftmuseum J. A. Dortmond
Singel 425, University Library
Trams: 1, 2, 4, 5, 9, 16, 24, 25
Open: Mon.–Fri. 10 a.m.–1 p.m., 2–4.30 p.m.
Guided tours by arrangement
The museum, named after the collector J. A. Dortmond, illustrates the development of the art of writing from about 3000 B.C. to the present day by means of objects and manuscripts. The handwriting department contains documentation on the art of writing

Schrijfmaschinemuseum (Typewriter museum)
Utrechtsestraat 70–72
Open: Mon.–Sat. 9 a.m.–5 p.m., Thurs. 9 a.m.–9 p.m.
Exhibition of old typewriters

Six Collectie
Amstel 218
Access only by letter of introduction from the Rijksmuseum (see Amsterdam A–Z, Rijksmuseum)
Private collection of 17th c. Dutch masters (including Rembrandt)

Spaarpottenmuseum (Museum of money boxes)
Raadhuisstraat 20
Trams: 13, 17; Buses 21, 67
Open: Mon.–Fri. 1–4 p.m., closed Sat., Sun. and public holidays
Admission fee
Private collection of more than 12,000 money boxes from all over the world

Stedelijk Museum
See Amsterdam A–Z, Stedelijk Museum

Peter Stuyvesant Stichting
Drentestraat 21
Buses: 23, 65, CN 173
Open: Mon.–Fri. 9 a.m.–noon and 1–4 p.m. (by prior arrangement)
Admission free
Exhibition of modern paintings and sculptures

Museums (cont.)

Nederlands Theaterinstituut
Herengracht 166
Trams: 13, 14, 17; Buses: 21, NC/GVB 67, CN 143 144, 145, 170, 171, 172
Open: daily except Mon. 11 a.m.–5 p.m.
Admission fee
The theatrical institute occupies five magnificent house in the Herengracht, the architecture and furnishing of which is alone worth a visit. The museum forms part of the institute. It presents the history of the Dutch theatre in drawings, sculptures, paintings, posters, props, etc. There are frequent temporary exhibitions

Tropenmuseum – see A–Z, Tropical Museum
Easily accessible to handicapped persons
Events: each 1st Sun. in month (except July-Sept.) performances on the Gamelan, a Javanese musical instrument. 25–27 Apr.: China Days
The children's museum, TM Junior, forms part of the museum. After renovation lasting nine months it was reopened in 1986 with the exhibition "The Hour of the Dragon" – about China, Hong Kong and the Chinese in the Netherlands. In addition special events are arranged, on weekdays for schools, at the weekends for all other children and young people

Uilenburg Restauratie Atelier (Restoration workshop)
Neiuwe Uilenburgerstraat 91. Tel. 22 84 56
Metro
Open by arrangement
Decorative Art

Verzetsmueum Amsterdam (Resistance museum)
Lekstraat 63 (in a former Jewish synagogue)
Trams: 4, 12, 25; Bus 15
Open: Tues.–Fri. 10 a.m.–5 p.m., Sat., Sun. and public holidays 1–5 p.m.
Admission fee
Museum of the Netherlands resistance movement during the German occupation 1940–1945.

Zoological Museum
Plantage Middenlaan 53
Trams: 6, 7, 9, 10, 14
Open: daily except Mon. 9.30 a.m.–4.30 p.m.; Guided tours by arrangement
In the Zoological Museum of the University of Amsterdam the collections include insects, mammals, birds, amphibians, reptiles, fishes, etc.

Museum of Land Reclamation

Although not strictly an Amsterdam Museum, many visitors may well be interested enough to visit this museum, in order to learn something of the great land-reclamation projects of the Netherlands. (see Facts and Figures, General, Polders in the Zuidersee, Deltaplan; A–Z Zuidersee)

Delta Plan

The Delta Expo on the Island of Neeltje Jans in the middle of the Oosterdchelde, where work on the project is directed, gives details of the construction of the greatest flood barrier in the world across the 9 km/5·6 mile-wide estuary of the Oosterscheld (eastern arm of the River Scheld)

Delta Expo
432826 Burgh–Haamstede
Bus: service bus from Dammansatz
Open: 1 Apr.–31 Oct.: daily 10 a.m.–5 p.m.; 1 Nov.–31 Mar.: Wed.–Sat. 10 a.m.–5 p.m.

Zuidersee

Zuiderseemuseum Enkhuizen (open-air museum)
Wierdijk 18
1601 LA Enkhuizen
Open: mid Apr.–mid Oct.: Mon.–Sat. 10 a.m.–5 p.m.
Admission fee

Music

Ballet and Opera

Amsterdam has two ballet companies of international reputation: the Netherlands National Ballet which includes both classical and modern works in its repertoire and the Nederlands Danz Theater which concentrates on contemporary ballet.
Until 1986, however, the city had no opera house of its own. Operas and also ballets were performed at the Stadsschouwburg. The gap has been filled by the opening of the new opera house "Het Muziektheater" on the Waterlooplein.

Theatres

Theatres for opera and ballet (selection):

Bellevue
Leidsekade 90. Tel. 24 72 48
Trams: 1, 2, 5

Shaffytheater
Keizersgracht 324. Tel. 23 13 11
Trams: 1, 2, 5, 13, 17

Stadsschouwburg
Leidseplein 26. Tel. 24 23 11
Tram: 1, 2, 5

Studio Danslab
Overamstelstraat 39. Tel. 26 71 08, 23 50 12

Concerts

Besides having the Concertgebouw Orchestra (see A–Z, Concertgebouw) Amsterdam has a good reputation as a music metropolis. There are many concert peformances in museums and churches which are very popular.

A selection of concert venues:

Amstelkring Museum
Oudezijds Voorburgwal 40. Tel. 24 66 04
Trams: 4, 9, 16, 24, 25

Carre
Amstel 115–125. Tel. 22 52 25
Tram: 4; Metro

Concertgebouw
Van Baerlestraat 98. Tel. 71 83 45
Trams: 2, 5, 16

De Engelse Kerk
Begijnof 48. Tel. 24 96 65
Trams: 1, 2, 5

Mozes en Aaronkerk
Waterlooplein 57. Tel. 22 13 05
Tram: 9; Metro

Nieuwe Kerk
Dam. Tel. 26 81 68
Trams: 1, 2, 4, 5, 9, 13, 16, 17, 24, 25

Oude Kerk
Oude Kerksplein 23. Tel. 24 91 83
Trams: 4, 9, 16, 24, 25

Sonesta Koepelzaal
Kattengat 1. Tel. 21 22 23
Trams: 1, 2, 5, 13, 17

Stedeljik Musem
Paulus Potterstraat 13. Tel. 5 73 29 11
Trams: 2, 3, 5, 12, 16; Buses: 26, 65, 66
Sept.–May, Saturday afternoon concerts of modern music, usually beginning at 3 p.m.

Waalse Kerk
O.Z. Achterbrugwal 157–159. Tel. 23 20 74
Trams: 4, 9, 16, 24, 25

Westerkerk
Prinsengracht 281. Tel. 24 77 66

De IJsbreker
Weeperzijde 23. Tel. 68 18 05
Metro

Jazz

See Cafés, Night Life

Night Life

Amsterdam's night life is concentrated in three centres. The oldest is situated around the port, in the Nieuwendijk and Zeedijk districts (see A–Z, Walletjes). Rembrandtplein and Thorbeckeplein are both surrounded by nightclubs – in almost every building in Thorbeckeplein there is a café, a bar, a nightclub or a cabaret. The floor-shows in these places are usually striptease. The third and newest amusement centre has become established in Leidseplein and its vicinity where there are also a number of discothèques. But hotel bars too are a favourite meeting place for "nightbirds". The following is just a small selection:

Bars

Halfmoon Bar (Amsterdam Hilton), Apollolaan 138.
Tel. 78 07 80
Apollo (Apollo Hotel), Apollolaan 2. Tel. 73 59 22
Golden Age Bar (Hotel Arthur Frommer), Noorderstraat 46.
Tel. 22 03 28

Brainbox Bar, Station Building Schiphol Airport. Tel. 15 21 50
Jonas Bar (Cok Hotel), Koningslaan 1. Tel. 64 61 11
Bass Pub (Doelen Crest Hotel), Nieuwe Doelenstraat 24. Tel. 22 07 22
Euromotel E9 Bar, Joan Muyskenweg 10. Tel. 65 81 81
Euromotel Schiphol Bar, Oude Haagseweg 20. Tel. 17 90 05
Le Bar (de l'Europe Hotel), Nieuwe Doelenstraat 2–4. Tel. 23 48 36
Pianobar Focus, Oudezijds Voorburgwal 189. Tel. 27 18 34
The Point (Golden Tulip Schiphol), Kruisweg 495, Hoofddorp. Tel. 02 503–158 51
Lobby Bar (Hotel Hilton Schiphol), Herbergierstraat, Schiphol Airport. Tel. 511 59 11
Library Bar (Marriott Hotel), Stadhouderskade 19–21. Tel. 83 51 51
The Pub (Novotel), Europaboulevard 10. Tel. 541 11 23
O'Henry's, Rokin 89. Tel. 25 14 98
Canal Bar (Okura Hotel), Ferd. Bolstraat 175. Tel. 78 71 11
The Old Bell, Rembrandtplein 46. Tel. 24 76 28
Palmbar (Krasnapolsky), Dam 9. Tel. 554 91 11
Pulitzer Bar (Hotel Pulitzer), Keizersgracht 234. Tel. 21 83 33
Patio Bar (Sonesta Hotel), Kattengat 1. Tel. 21 22 23
U.B.Q., P.C. Hooftstraat 100. Tel. 72 90 04
Tasmanbar (Victoria Hotel), Damrak 1–6. Tel. 23 42 55

With Live Music

Alto, Korte Leidsedwarsstraat 115. Tel. 26 32 49
Amstel Hotel Bar, Prof. Tulpplein 1. Tel. 22 60 60 (closed Sun. and Mon.)
Bamboo Bar, Lange Leidsedwarstraat 64. Tel. 24 39 93
Cab Kay's Jazz Piano Bar, Beulingstraat 9. Tel. 23 35 94 (closed Sun. and Mon.)
Clock Bar (Crest Hotel), De Boelelaan 2. Tel. 42 98 55 (closed Sun.)
Joseph Lam Jazzclub, v. Diemenstraat 8. Tel. 22 80 86 (closed Mon. and Thurs.)
Pianobar le Maxim, Leidekruisstraat 35. Tel. 24 19 20
Ciel Bleu Bar (Okura Hotel), Ferd. Bolstraat 175. Tel. 78 71 11
The String, Nes 98. Tel. 25 90 15

Discothèques

Boston Club (Sonesta Hotel), Kattengat 1. Tel. 24 55 61
Juliana's, Apollolaan 138–140. Tel. 73 73 13
Mazzo, Rozengracht 114. Tel. 26 75 00
'T Okshoofd, Herengracht 114. Tel. 22 76 85
De Schakel, Korte Leidsedwarsstraat 49. Tel. 22 76 85
Zorba de Buddha Rajneesh, O.Z. Voorburgwal 216. Tel. 25 96 42

Cafés

See entry

Closing Time

Closing time is 1 a.m.

Parks

Amsterdamse Bos
The Amsterdamse Bos stands out from Amsterdam's 20 or so other parks, with its vast woods and many facilities for recreation (riding, camping, walking, etc.), stretching as far as Amstelveen (see Amsterdam A–Z, Amsterdamse Bos).

Bar in Amsterdam

On the Walletjes – the red light district (see Amsterdam A–Z)

Beatrixpark
next to the RAI congress centre

Erasmuspark
on the Jan van Galenstraat

Hortus Botanicus UVA (Botanic Garden of Amsterdam University)
See A–Z Hortus Botanicus

Hortus Botanicus VU (Botanic Garden of the Free University)
Van der Boechorststraat 8
Buses: 23, 65, CN 173
Open: Mon.–Fri. 8 a.m.–4.15 p.m.
Admission free

Julianapark
Prins Bernhardplein

Oosterpark
near the Singelgracht

Rembrandtspark
on the Einsteinweg (A10)

Vondelpark
See Amsterdam A–Z, Vondelpark

Westerpark
on the Haarlemmervaart

Pawnbroker (Pandjeshuis)

Municipal Pawnbroker

Oudezijds Voorburgwal 300. Tel. 22 24 21

Petrol

Since April 1986 ordinary leaded petrol is no longer sold in the Netherlands. Drivers who use normal leaded petrol (two-star) must change to Super.

Pets

Certificate of Vaccination

Dogs and cats can be taken into the Netherlands if they have a certificate of vaccination against rabies not less than a month or more than a year old. (In view of the quarantine regulations on re-entry into Britain most British visitors will of course leave their pets at home.)

Police

Police Headquarters

Elandsgracht 117. Tel. 5 59 91 11
Trams: 1, 2 5; Bus: 67

Lijnbaansgracht/Corner Elandsgracht. Tel. 5 59 23 03
Trams: 1, 2 5; Bus: 67

Warmoesstraat 44–46. Tel. 5 59 22 03
Trams: 1, 2, 4, 5, 9, 13, 16, 17, 24, 25

Alarm (SOS Emergency Call)

The police can be reached at any time of the day or night by dialling 22 22 22

Post

Head Post Office

Nieuwezijds Voorburgwal 182. Tel. 5 55 89 11
Trams: 1, 2, 5, 13, 17; Buses: 21, 67
Open: Mon.–Fri. 8.30 a.m.–6 p.m., Thurs. 8.30 a.m.–8.30 p.m., Sat. 9 a.m.–noon
For long distance phone calls and telegrams open 24 hours daily via the entrance at the rear

Parcel Post

Oosterdokskade Post Office
Open: Mon.–Fri. 8.30 a.m.–8.30 p.m., Sat. 9 a.m.–noon

Times of Opening

Amsterdam's other post offices are open from Monday to Friday between 9 a.m. and 5 p.m.

Postal Rates

Letters inside the EEC: 0·75 hfl, otherwise 0.90 hfl
Postcards inside the EEC: 0·55 hfl, otherwise 0.65 hfl

Programme of Events

The VVV publishes "Amsterdam This Week" which is a weekly paper in English giving details of all events in Amsterdam (obtainable from all VVV offices and large hotels).
Information in Dutch is published in "Aktueel Amsterdam" (available from bookshops) and "Amsterdam Uitkrant" (monthly publication available from the Stadsshouwburg).

Public Holidays/Commemorations

Public Holidays

New Year, Good Friday (most shops are open), Easter, the Queen's Birthday (30 April, most shops are closed), Ascension Day, Whitsun, Christmas.

Commemorations

4 May (for the victims of the Second World War, not a public holiday), 5 May (Liberation day; most shops are open).

Public Transport

Amsterdam has a widespread public-transport network. Most people travel by bus or tram as the building of the underground network was halted after the first stretch was completed due to massive local opposition on the grounds of its anticipated harmful impact on the environment.

There are now two lines serving 20 stations. Buses, trams and the Metro run until midnight, after which night buses operate.

Co-ordinated Transport Undertaking

All public transport timetables and fares are co-ordinated. There are controlled by the GVB Gemeentevervoerbedrijk Amsterdam), the city transport undertaking. The city is divided into zones, with separate tariffs. The fare depends on the length of the journey to be undertaken and the number of zones through which the passenger passes. The division of zones is shown at all stations and stops.

Ticket strips

There are no longer any single tickets, only the so-called "strip tickets" (strippenkaart). Having discovered from the plan at the station or stop through how many zones the proposed journey passes, the passenger has the required number of strips cancelled by the conductor of the tram or bus, or by an automatic machine on the Metro. The smallest "strippenkaart" covers six journeys in the city centre by bus, tram or Metro. There are also tickets with 10 and 15 "strips".

Day Tickets

However, for visitors it is far simpler and more convenient to buy a day ticket. This costs 8·4 hfl. (1986) and is valid for one whole day and the following night on all buses, trams and the Metro. The day ticket can be obtained at the GVB Information and Ticket Office in front of the Main Station and in the "Bulldog" Information Café on the Leidseplein as well as from all tram- and bus-drivers.

Tickets for 2, 3 or more days

Since it is always wiser not to use one's car in Amsterdam (parking problems, theft, etc.), but to rely on public transport, the visitor staying several days is advised to purchase a ticket covering 2, 3 or more days. These are also obtainable at the GVB office outside the Main Station, or at the "Bulldog" Café on the Leidseplein. A two-day ticket costs 11·25 hfl. and a three-day ticket 13·8 hfl. For each further day the price rises by 2·6 hfl. (prices in 1986).

60-Minute Ticket

A 60-minute ticket is obtainable from bus and tram conductors.

Information

Detailed information on all aspects of public transport can be obtained at the GVB Information and Ticket Office outside the Main Station and at the "Bulldog" Café on the Leidesplein: open Mon.–Fri. 7 a.m.–11 p.m., Sat. and Sun. 8 a.m.–11 p.m. Telephone enquiries (7 a.m.–11 p.m.) 27 27 27.

GVB Welcoming Prospectus

In hotels, at the above-mentioned GVB Offices, at the GVB desk at Amstel Station or at the GVB Main Agency, Prins Hendrikkade 108–110, a free "welcoming prospectus" can be obtained; this gives useful advice about public transport and includes a plan of Amsterdam.

Excursions

Since public transport in the whole of the Netherlands is divided into zones and since the fare for each zone is the same for all transport undertakings, the Nationale Strippenkaart (national strip ticket) is most suitable for excursions. It is obtainable from stations, both transport undertakings, post offices, and many VVV offices (see Information), and can be purchased in advance. With this ticket the visitor can make use of all bus, tram and Metro lines in the Netherlands. The ticket consists of 15 strips.

Radio/Television

In line with the Dutch attitude that everyone should be free to express themselves, radio and television is in the hands of a number of private stations who put together widely differing programmes reflecting their religious or political views.
These Radio/TV associations are funded by their members' contributions which corresponds to the amount of time the stations get on the air. There are, among others, Protestant (EO), Catholic (KRO) and Socialist (VARA) stations as well as the independent state-financed Nederlandse Omroep Stichting with its headquarters in Hilversum.

Restaurants

Set Meal Prices

The prices for a set meal (menu) in Amsterdam restaurants can be approximately divided into three categories:
upper price category over 50 hfl
medium price category 30–50 hfl
lower price category 18·75–30 hfl

Upper Price Category

De Bols Taverne, Rozengracht 106. Tel. 24 57 52
Open: Mon.–Fri. from noon, Sat. from 5 p.m.
Closed: Sun.; 25, 26, 31 Dec.

Excelsior (Hotel de l'Europe), Nieuwe Doelenstraat 2–4.
Tel. 23 48 36
Open: from 12.30 and 7 p.m.

De Kersentuin (Garden Hotel), Dysselhofplantsoen 7.
Tel. 64 21 21
Open: Mon.–Fri. from noon and 6 p.m., Sat. from 6 p.m.
Closed: Sun.; 24 Dec., 1 Jan.

Mart Inn, Havenrestaurant, De Ruyterkade 7. Tel. 25 62 77
Open: daily from 11.30 a.m. and 6 p.m.
Closed: 24–26 and 31 Dec., 1 Jan.

Le Reflet d'Or (Grand Hotel Krasnapolsky), Dam 9.
Tel. 5 54 91 11
Open: daily from noon

Rosarium, Parkrestaurant, Amstelpark 1, Europaboulevard.
Tel. 44 40 85
Open: Mon.–Fri. from 9 a.m., Sat. from 6 p.m.
Closed: Sun.; 24, 31 Dec. 1 Jan.

French Cuisine

Ciel Bleu (Okura Hotel), Ferd. Bolstraat 175. Tel. 78 71 11
Open: daily from 6.30 p.m.

De Goudsbloem (Hotel Pulitzer), Reestraat 8. Tel. 25 32 88
Open: Mon.–Fri. from noon and 6 p.m., Sat., Sun. from 6 p.m.
Closed: 24, 31 Dec.

Rib Room Restaurant (Sonesta Hotel) Kattengat 1.
Tel. 21 22 23
Open: Mon.–Fri. from noon and 6 p.m., Sat. from 6 p.m.

La Rive (Amstel Hotel), Prof. Tulpplein 1. Tel. 22 60 60
Open: daily from noon and 6 p.m.
Closed: 24, 25, 31 Dec.

Medium Price Category

Brasserie van Baerle, Van Baerlestraat, 158. Tel. 79 15 32
Open: Mon.–Fri. from 11 a.m., Sun. from 10 a.m.
Closed: Sat., 5, 24–26, 31 Dec., 1 Jan.

Le Clown, Koningstraat 29. Tel. 26 82 90
Open: Tues.–Sat. from 6 p.m.
Closed: Sun., Mon.; 5, 31 Dec., 1 Jan.

Four Seasons (Caransa Crest Hotel), Rembrandtplein 19.
Tel. 22 94 55
Open: from noon and 6 p.m.

Le Grill (Novotel Amsterdam), Europaboulevard 10.
Tel. 5 41 11 23
Open: from 6.30 p.m.

De Groene Lanteerne, Haarlemmerstraat 43. Tel. 24 19 52
Open: Tues.–Fri. from noon and 5 p.m., Sat from 5 p.m.
Closed: Sun., Mon.; 5, 24–26, 31 Dec., 1 Jan., July

The Lantern (Amsterdam Crest Hotel), De Boelelaan 2.
Tel. 46 23 00
Open: from noon and 6 p.m.

Miranda Paviljoen, Amsteldijk 223. Tel. 44 57 68
Open: from noon
Closed: 1 Jan.

De Muzen (Apollofirsthotel), Apollolaan 123–125.
Tel. 79 79 71
Open: from 6.30 p.m.
Closed: 5, 24–26, 31 Dec., 1 Jan.

Oranjehof (Hotel Arthur Frommer), Noorderstraat 26.
Tel. 22 03 28
Open: from 6 p.m.

Paviljoen (Apollo Hotel), Apollolaan 2. Tel. 73 59 22
Open: from noon and 6 p.m.
Closed: 24, 31 Dec.

De Prinsenkelder, Prinsengracht 438. Tel. 26 77 21

Rembrandt, P.C. Hooftstraat 31. Tel. 62 90 11
Open: Tues.–Sun. from noon
Closed: 5, 25, 26 Dec., 1 Jan.

Van Riebeeck (Victoria Hotel), Damrak 1–6. Tel. 23 42 55
Open: from noon and 6 p.m.
Closed: 24, 25, 31 Dec.

Henri Smits, Beethovenstraat 55. Tel. 79 17 06
Open: Mon.–Sat. from 10 a.m., Sun. from 5 p.m.
Closed: 25, 26 Dec.

Warstein, Spuistraat 266. Tel. 22 96 09
Open: Tues.–Sat. from 5 p.m.
Closed: Mon.; 25, 26, 31 Dec.

French Cuisine

Le Dauphin (Memphis Hotel), De Lairessestraat 87.
Tel. 73 31 41
Open: from noon and 6 p.m.

La Belle Epoque, Leidselplein 14. Tel. 23 83 61
Open: from noon and 5 p.m.
Closed: 25, 26, 31 Dec.

Bistro La Forge, Lorte Leidsedwarsstraat, 26. Tel. 24 00 95
Open: from 5 p.m.
Closed: 31 Dec.

De Hartedief, Hartenstraat 24. Tel. 25 85 00
Open: Mon.–Fri. from noon and 5.30 p.m., Sat., Sun. from 2 p.m.
Closed: 24, 31 Dec.

De Kelderhof, Prinsengracht 494. Tel. 22 06 82
Open: from 5 p.m.
Closed: 5, 24, 31 Dec.

'T Prinsengatje, Prinsengracht 604. Tel. 25 13 40
Open: Tues.–Sun. from 6 p.m.
Closed: 5, 24–26, 31 Dec., 1 Jan.

Lower Price Category

City Hotel, Prins Hendrikkade 130. Tel. 23 08 36
Openm: from noon and 6 p.m.

Fidelio (Hotel Beethoven), Beethovenstraat 41–43.
Tel. 64 48 16
Open: from noon

Kameleon, O.Z. Voorburgwal 248. Tel. 24 44 61
Open: from 11 a.m. and 5 p.m.
Closed: 5, 24–26, 31 Dec., 1 Jan.

Napoleon Hotel, Valkenburgerstraat 72–74. Tel. 26 03 23
Open: from 7.30 p.m.

Smits Koffiehuis, Stationsplein 10. Tel. 23 37 77
Open: Mon.–Sat. from 8 a.m., Sun. from 9 a.m.
Closed: 1 Jan.

De Suikerhof, Prinsengracht 381. Tel. 22 75 71
Open: Wed.–Sun. from 5.30 p.m.
Closed: Mon., Tues.; 5, 24–26, 31 Dec., 1 Jan.

De Triangel (Hotel Trianon), J.W. Browersstraat 3–7.
Tel. 73 30 73
Open: from noon and 4 p.m.

Tourist Menu

Restaurants with this sign offer a three-course meal at an inclusive price of 18·75 hfl. (1986). Among these restaurants are:

American Hotel, Leidseplein 24–28. Tel. 24 53 22
Open: from 10.30 a.m.

The Captain's Inn, Damrak 57. Tel. 22 00 20
Open: from 11.30 a.m.
Closed: 24–26, 31 Dec., 1 Jan.

Euromotel Schiphol, Oude Haagseweg 20. Tel. 17 90 05
Open: from noon

Haesje Claes, N.Z. Voorburgwal 320. Tel. 24 99 98
Open: Mon.–Sat. from 11 a.m., Sun. from 5 p.m.

Heineken Hoeg, Kleine Gartmanplantsoen 1–3.
Tel. 23 07 00
Open: from 11 a.m.
Closed: 31 Dec.

Rhapsody, Rembrandtplein 7. Tel. 26 22 46
Open: from 11.30 a.m.
Closed: 25 Dec.

De Roode Leeuw (Hotel), Damrak 93–94. Tel. 24 03 96
Open: from 9 a.m.

De Serre (Sonesta Hotel), Kattengat 1. Tel. 21 22 23
Open: from 6.30 a.m.

Oud Holland, N.Z. Voorburgwal 105. Tel. 24 68 48
Open: Mon.–Sat. from noon
Closed: Sun., 25, 31 Dec., 1 Jan., July/Aug.

Norway Inn, Kalverstraat 65–69. Tel. 26 23 26
Open: from noon
Closed: 1 Jan.

Netherlands Cuisine

In restaurants with the sign "Neerlands Dis" Dutch specialities are featured:

Bodega Keyzer, Van Baerlestraat 96. Tel. 71 14 41
Open: Mon.–Sat. from noon
Closed: Sun.; 25, 26 Dec., 1 Jan.

Mistral (Parkhotel) Stadhouderskade 25. Tel. 71 74 74
Open: from 5 p.m.

Dutch Corner (Hotel Okura), Ferd. Bolstraat 175.
Tel. 78 71 71
Open: from 7 a.m.

Die Port van Cleve, N.Z. Voorburgwal 178–180. Tel. 24 00 47
Open: from noon

Dutch dishes are also served in:

Dorrius, N.Z. Voorburgwal 336–342. Tel. 23 52 45

In de Gerstekorrel, Damstraat 22. Tel. 24 13 67

't Heertje, Herenstraat 16. Tel. 25 81 27

Snacks

Eetsalon van Dobben, Korte Reguliersdwarsstraat 5–9.
Tel. 24 42 00
Open: Mon.–Sat. from 9.30 a.m., Sun. from 11.30 a.m.
Closed: 25 Dec.

Herring Dishes

't Haringhuis, Oude Doelenstraat 18. Tel. 22 12 84

Haringhandel Visser, Muntplein Haringker

Pancakes

Pannekoekhuisje Bredero, O.Z. Voorburgwal 244.
Tel. 22 94 61
Open: from 11.30 a.m.–7.30 p.m.
Closed: 5, 24, 25, 31 Dec.

Pancake Bakery, Prinsengracht 191. Tel. 25 13 33
Open: from noon
Closed: 25, 26 Dec.

Pannekoekhuis, Prinsengracht 332. Tel. 22 36 28
Open: Wed.–Sun. from noon
Closed: Mon., Tues.; 5, 25, 26,31 Dec., 1 Jan.

Fish Restaurants

Albatros Seefood House, Westerstraat 264. Tel. 27 99 32
Open: Mon.–Sat. from 6 p.m.
Closed: Sun.; 5, 24–26, 31 Dec., 1 Jan.

Julia, Amstelveenseweg 160. Tel. 79 53 94
Open: Mon., Wed.–Sun. from 5 p.m.
Closed: Tues.; 5, 24, 31 Dec.

De Oesterbar, Leidseplein 10. Tel. 26 34 63
Open: from noon
Closed: 24–26 Dec.

Sluizer, Utrechtsestraat 43–45. Tel. 26 35 57

Night Restaurant

Kiekeboe, Vondelstraat 63a. Tel. 12 30 21
Open: from 10 p.m.
Closed: 24 Dec.–7 Jan.

Vegetarian Restaurant

Baldur, Weteringschans 76. Tel. 24 46 72
Open: Mon.–Sat. from 5 p.m.
Closed: Sun.; 24–26, 31 Dec., 1 Jan.

Golden Temple, Utrechtsestraat 126. Tel. 26 85 60
Open: from 11 a.m. and 5 p.m.
Closed: 25 Dec., 1 Jan.

It is said that in Amsterdam one can eat in any language; here is a small selection:

Chinese Cuisine

China Corner, Damstraat 1. Tel. 22 88 16
Open: from noon

Dynasty, Reguliersdwarsstraat, 30. Tel. 26 84 00
Open: Mon. Wed.–Sun. from 5.30 p.m.
Closed: Tues.; 25–26, 31 Dec., 1 Jan.

Indonesian Cuisine

Bali, Leidseplein 89–97. Tel. 22 78 78
Open: from noon and 6 p.m.
Closed: 5, 12, 24, 31 Dec., 1 Jan.

Sama Sebo, P. C. Hooftstraat 27. Tel. 62 81 46
Open: Mon.–Sat. from noon and 6.30 p.m.
Closed: Sun.; 22 Dec., 1 Jan.

Speciaal, Nieuwe Leliestraat 142. Tel. 24 97 06
Open: from 5.30 p.m.
Closed: 5, 24, 25, 31 Dec.

Japanese Cuisine

Kei, Apollolaan 138–140. Tel. 78 07 80
Open: Mon.–Fri. from noon and 6.30 p.m., Sat. and Sun. from 6.30 p.m.
Closed: 1 Jan.

Teppan Yaki Steakhouse (Okura Hotel), Ferd. Bolstraat 175. Tel. 78 71 11
Open: from noon and 6 p.m.

Caribbean Cuisine

Rum Runners, Prinsengracht 277. Tel. 27 40 79
Open: Mon.–Sat. from noon and 6 p.m., Sun. from 1 p.m.
Closed: 25 Dec.

Mexican Cuisine

Rose's Cantina, Reguliersdwarsstraat 38. Tel. 25 97 97

Spanish Cuisine

Vamos-a-Ver, Govert Flinckstraat 308. Tel. 73 69 92

Shopping Streets

Jordaan

Between Prinsengracht and Lijnbaansgracht. Small shops and boutiques selling second-hand goods, bric-à-brac and collector's items.

Kalverstraat

Mainly shoe shops and clothing boutiques.

P. C. Hooftstraat

High fashion, exclusive shops of all kinds.

Utrechtsestraat

A mecca for the gourmet.

Sightseeing

Boat Trips on the Canals

No visitor should leave Amsterdam without going for a trip on the canals in one of more than 65 glass-topped boats that take you on a tour of the canals, out on to the Amstel and round the harbour. It is also quite an experience to make the trip at night. Boats leave every hour in the summer months and at longer intervals in the winter. The trips last from between an hour and half a day and can be booked at the Amsterdam tourist information centre (VVV, see Information).

Operators

Reederei Lovers B.V.
Prins Hendrikkade 25–27
Opposite the Central Station. Tel. 22 21 81 or 25 93 23
Suitable for people in wheelchairs

Holland International
Prins Hendrikkade
Opposite the Central Station. Tel. 22 77 88

Reederei Noord-Zuid
Stadhouderskade 25. Tel. 79 13 70

Reederei Kooij
Rokin near Spui. Tel. 23 38 10 or 23 41 86

Reederei Plas
Damrak near Central Station. Tel. 24 54 06 or 22 60 96

Bus Tours

Guided tours round Amsterdam or local excursions can be booked with the following operators (or at the VVV tourist information centre):

Holland International Travel Group, Rokin 54
Holland Travel Service, Rokin 9
Key Tours, Dam 19
Lindbergh Travel Bureau, Damrak 26

Excursions include trips to the fishing villages of Marken and Volendam, the cheese market in Alkmaar, the bulbfields and the Keukenhof, The Hague, Delft and the Zuider Zee (see Amsterdam A–Z, under the appropriate headings).

Boat trip on the canals

Practical Information

Sightseeing	The Dutch airline KLM (Tel. 49 36 33) arranges half-hour sightseeing flights over Amsterdam every Sat. from April to October. Price: adults about 50 hfl; children about 45 hfl.
Grachtenfiets (pedal bikes)	By using grachtenfiets (canal bikes), which are pedal bikes for two to four persons, Amsterdam's canals can be explored on an individual basis. In a brochure, which the hirer of such a craft is given, the "rules of the game" are laid down – there are, of course, other craft on the canals – and four possible routes are described; the advantage is that the boat does not have to be returned to the place from which it has been hired.
Mooring Places	Leidseplein (between Marriott Hotel and American Hotel) Between the Rijksmuseum and the Heineken Brewery Prinsengracht at the Westerkerk (near the Anne Frank House) Keizersgracht/corner of Leidsestraat Open: daily 9 a.m.–11 p.m.

Specialist Shops

Antiques	See Antiques
Camping Equipment	Gaasper camping, Loosdrechtsedreef 7 Kampeerterrein Amsterdam Bos (camp site) Neef Sport, Raadhuisstraat 32
Cheese	Abraham Kef, Marnixstraat 192 (Here you can sample the cheeses with a glass of wine) De Ark, Jacob van Campenstraat 35 (Here you can see cheese being made and stored)
Chemists (Drogisterij)	Jacob Hooij & Co., Kloveniersburgwal 12 (old-fashioned chemist's shop) B. Heinhuis, Spuistraat 58 Marjo, Zeedijk 68 Tijhuis, Claas van Maarssenplein 37
Clogs	't Klompenhuisje, Nieuwe Hoogstraat 917 Open: daily 11 a.m.–6 p.m. De Klompenboer, N.Z. Voorburgwal 20 Clockwitz, Herengracht 305 A. W. G. Otten, Albert Cuypstraat 102
Coffee Roasting	Geels en Co., Warmoesstraat 67
Cookery Books	De Kookboekhandel, Runstraat 26 Open: Tues., Wed., Fri. 8 a.m.–6 p.m., Thurs. noon–9 p.m., Sat. 11 a.m.–5 p.m.
Cosmetics	De Driehoek, Martelaarsgracht 18 Duffels, International Cosmetics Buitenveldertselaan 36
Delft Porcelain, Cristal and Chinoiserie	Focke & Meltzer, Kalverstraat 176 Van Gelder, Van Baerlestraat 40 Kado Boutique Exclusive, Hoofdweg 478 Het Kristalhuis, Rozenboomsteeg 12–14 Porcella, Hugo de Vrieslaan 45 Roenthal Studio House, Heiligeweg 49–51 Wille & Co., Nieuwendijk 216–218

Delicatessen

Dikker & Thijs, Leidsestraat 82

Diamond Cutting

See Diamonds

Jewellers

Schaap en Citroen, Kalverstraat 1 and Rokin 12
Bernard Schipper, Kalverstraat 36–38
Elka Watch, Kalverstraat 206
Smit Ouwerkerk, Singel 320
Hans Appenzeller, Grimburgwal 1 (modern costume jewellery)

Jewellers with Diamond Cutting

Amstel Diamonds, Amstel 208. Tel. 23 15 41
Open: Mon.–Sat. 9 a.m.–5 p.m.; Nov.–Mar. Sat. 9 a.m.–1 p.m.
Trams: 4, 9

Diamonds Direct Herman Schipper B.V., Heiligeweg 3.
Tel. 24 96 16
Open: Mon.–Sat. 9 a.m.–6 p.m., Thurs. also 7–9 p.m.
Trams: 1, 2, 5

The Mill Diamonds, Rokin 123. Tel. 23 85 04
Open: Mon.–Fri. 9 a.m.–6 p.m., Sat. 9 a.m.–5 p.m.
Trams: 4, 9, 16, 24, 25

Willem van Pampus Diamond Center, Kalverstraat 117.
Tel. 23 68 98
Open: daily 9.30 a.m.–5.30 p.m., Thurs. 9.30 a.m.–8.30 p.m.;
Oct.–Mar. Sun. 11 a.m.–5.30 p.m.
Trams 4, 9, 16, 24, 25

Kitchen Utensils

Brigette's Boutique, Amstel 328
Pots and pans as well as enormous old stoves and tiny doll's house cookers

Metz & Co., Keizersgracht/corner of Leidsestraat
Kitchen boutique as well as furniture, clothes, fabrics, handicrafts

Linen

Het Kantenhuis, Kalverstraat 124

Pearls

Andre Coppenhagen, Bloemgracht 38

Souvenirs

Portobello Giftshop, Rokin 107
Rally Wachtel, Damstraat 6
Rozengalerie, Rozengracht 75
Contemporary glassware
De Voetboog art, Voetboogsteeg 16
Art and handcrafted work
A. Smit, Buikslotermeerplein 254
The Turquoise Tomahawk, Berenstraat 16

Tobacconists

P. C. G. Hajenisu, Rokin 92 (Purveyor to the Royal Household)
A. M. van Lookeren, Beethovenstraat 88
J. van Beek, Nieuwendijk 109
J. Naarden, Damstraat 2a

Tulips

Wys, Singel 508 (flower market)
Tulip bulbs and other plants for sale and despatch

Opening Times

Shops are usually open from Monday to Friday from 9 a.m. to 6 p.m. (Thurs. until 9 p.m., Sat. until 5 p.m.). They have their own morning or afternoon closing time (sometimes a whole day per week). Often this is on Monday morning

Sport

Football	Ajax-Stadion, Middenweg Olympia-Stadion, Stadionplein
Bowling	Bowling Centre Knijn, Scheldeplein 3 Tram: 25
Golf	Golfclub Olympus, "Over-Amstel", Jan Vroegopsingel
Miniature Golf	There are miniature golf courses in the Amstelpark, the Amsterdamse Bos and the Sloterpark
Skating	Jaap Edenbaan Radioweg 64 Tram: 9 Open: Oct.–March. Open in winter on the Leidseplein
Tennis	Frans Ottenstadion Stadionstraat 10 Also squash facilities
Swimming	See Swimming Pools
Riding	Amsterdamse Manege, Amsterdamse Bos
Rowing	Jachthaven Neptunus, Amsterdamse Bos Rowing boats for hire
Sailing	Jachthaven Waterlust, Amsterdamse Bos Sailing boats for hire
Surfing	Saasperplas Metro Sloterplas Tram: 1

Stations

Amsterdam's main station, Centraal Station, is situated in the city centre (see A–Z, Centraal Station).
The information office is open Mon.–Fri. 8 a.m.–10 p.m., Sat., Sun. and public holidays 9 a.m.–6 p.m. Telephone 23 83 83 Mon.–Fri. 8 a.m.–10 p.m., Sat., Sun and public holidays 9 a.m.–10 p.m.

Other stations

Amstel Station, Julianaplein
Muiderport Station, Oosterpoortplein
Amsterdam RAI, Europaboulevard
Amsterdam Zuid, World Trade Center

Swimming Pools (open Luchtbaden/Overdektebaden)

Outdoor Pools

Bredius, Spaarndammerdijk.
Flevopark, Zeeburgerdijk 230.
Florapark, Sneeuwbalweg 5.
Jan van Galen, Jan van Galenstraat 315.
De Mirandabad, De Mirandalaan 9.
Sloterpark, Sloterplas.

Indoor Pools

Florapark, Sneeuwbalweg 5.
Heiligeweg, Neiligeweg 19.
Marnixbad, Marnixplein 9.
Mirandabad (including pool with wave-making machine), De Mirandalaan 9.
Sloterparkbad, Slotermeerlaan 2.

Saunas

De Driehoek, Martelaarsgracht 18. Tel. 27 36 36
Open: daily

Sauna Kylpy
for ladies and married couples:
Mercatorplein 25. Tel. 12 34 96
Open: for ladies Mon.–Fri. 10 a.m.–6 p.m.; for couples Sat. 10 a.m.–6 p.m., Tues. 5–11 p.m. for men: Damrak 54.
Tel. 22 60 12
Open: Mon.–Fri. 10 a.m.–11 p.m.; Sat. 10 a.m.–6 p.m.

Spafit (Fitness Centre), Leidsegracht 84. Tel. 24 25 12
Splash Fitness Club, Looiersgracht 26–30. Tel. 24 84 44
Splash Sonesta Fitness Club, Kattengat 1. Tel. 27 10 44

Taxis

Taxi Phone Numbers

Taxis can be ordered by ringing 77 77 77.

Fare

The fare is made up of a basic charge plus a kilometre supplement and Amsterdam also has the usual day and night rates. The tip is included in the fare but the driver will not object if cents are rounded up to the nearest guilder.

Telephone

Dialling Codes

In common with most European countries, the Netherlands has an STD dialling system for national and international telephone calls.
In the Netherlands the international dialling prefix is 09. To make an international call, first dial the international prefix (09), then the country code (61 for Australia, 1 for Canada and the USA, 27 for South Africa and 44 for the UK), followed by the area code (minus the first 0 for the UK) and the local number.

International Calls from a Telephone Box

When making an international call from a phone box the following points should be noted:
Have sufficient coins (25 cent, 2·50 guilder) ready.
After inserting a coin (at least 25 cents) wait for the disengaged signal; then dial the international code 09; wait once more for the disengaged tone. As soon as this is heard dial the country code, the area code, following by the subscriber's number (omitting the first 0).
When necessary insert further coins.

International Information

Tel. 0018

Operator-connected Calls

Tel. 0010

Charge for Local Calls

A local call costs 25 cents.

Information

For help with telephoning consult the leaflet giving telephone and postal charges available from all post offices.

Theatres

Theater de Brakke Grond, Nes 53–55. Tel. 24 03 94
Trams: 4, 9, 16, 24, 25
Performances also in English

Theater Carré, Amstel 115–125. Tel. 22 52 25
Tram: 4; Metro
Amsterdam's largest theatre – plays, cabaret, music and dance (no fixed programme)

Cleyntheater (Nieuwendam), H. Cleyndertweg 63A.
Tel. 37 18 15
Bus: 33

Theater de Engelenbak, Nes 71. Tel. 26 36 44/23 57 23

De Kleine Komedie, Amstel 55–58. Tel. 24 05 34
Trams: 4, 9, 16, 24, 25

De Meervaart, Osdorpplein 67. Tel. 10 73 93
Tram: 1

Mickery, Rozengracht 117. Tel. 23 67 77
Trams: 13, 17
Experimental theatre with foreign companies

Nieuwe de la Mar Theater, Marnixstraat 404. Tel. 23 34 62
Trams: 1, 2, 5

De Populier, Nieuwe Herengracht 93. Tel. 24 31 36
Tram: 9; Metro

Shaffytheater, Keizersgracht 324. Tel. 23 13 11
Trams: 1, 2, 5, 13, 17

Stadsschouwburg, Leidseplein 26. Tel. 24 23 11
Trams: 1, 2, 5
Amsterdam's most beautiful theatre, mainly plays but also opera and ballet

Theater de Suikerhof, Prinsengracht 381. Tel. 22 75 71
Trams; 13, 17

Theater Tingel Tangel, Nieuwezijds Voorburgwal 282.
Tel. 26 46 95
Trams: 1, 2, 5

Children's Theatre

Diridas Poppentheater
Hobbemakade 68. Tel. 62 15 88
Tram: 16

Circus Elleboog
Passeerdersgracht 32. Tel. 26 93 70
Tram: 17

Amstelveens Poppentheater
Wolfert van Borsselenweg 85a. Tel. 45 04 39
Buses: 146, 147, 170, 171/172

Kinderfilmcentrum
Ceintuurbaan 338. Tel. 62 34 88
Tram: 24

De Rietwijker
Parlevinker 9. Tel. 33 13 37
Bus: 34

Poppentheater Musquit
Rechtboomsloot 42. Tel. 26 40 15
Metro

Time

Dutch Summertime – i.e. Central European Time (CET) plus one hour – operates from the beginning of April to the end of September.

Times of Opening

Chemists

Mon.–Sat. 8 a.m.–5.30 p.m.

Banks

Mon.–Fri. 9 a.m.–4 p.m.

Shops

Shops are open as a rule from 9 a.m. to 6 p.m. during the week and until 5 p.m. on Saturdays. Most shops stay open until 9 p.m. on Thursdays and they usually close in the lunch-hour, as well closing for a morning or an afternoon and sometimes a whole day once a week.

Department stores and supermarkets usually do not open on Mondays until 1.30 p.m. and most butchers are closed on Mondays.

Although shops stay open late on Thursdays until 9 p.m., they often also close for an hour between 6 and 7 p.m.

Department Stores

Times of opening are the same as for the other shops. They stay open in the lunch-hour but are usually closed on Monday mornings.

Churches

Many churches are open only during services. The verger should be contacted at other times.

Post Offices

Mon.–Fri. 9 a.m.–5 p.m.

Time to Travel

Amsterdam is worth a visit at any time of the year but it is especially worth visiting in the spring when the parks and bulbfields are in full bloom. In the autumn the city and countryside are bathed in the same light as depicted in the paintings of the Dutch Old Masters.

Tipping (Fooi)

In the Netherlands tipping is usually for special services only (10–15%), but it has become common practice to round up cents to the nearest guilder in restaurants, cafés, hotels and taxis.

Tourist Information

See Information

Traffic

Drinking and Driving

In the Netherlands the legal limit for alcohol in the blood is 0·5 part per millilitre. Anyone visiting Amsterdam's many cafés is advised to leave his car behind at the hotel.

Vehicle Thefts

It is advisable to make sure your vehicle is securely locked and that nothing of value is left in the car.

Speed Limits

On motorways: 100 km/62 miles per hour.
Outside built-up areas: 80 km/50 miles per hour.
In built-up areas: 50 km/30 miles per hour.
In "quiet" zones (signed by a white house on a blue ground): walking-pace.

Lighting

Main beam or dipped headlights must be used from half an hour after sunset until one hour before sunrise. During daylight hours the use of lights is compulsory if weather conditions make it necessary. Main beams may not be used in built-up areas if there is adequate public lighting, outside built-up areas on roads with adequate public lighting at regular intervals, when facing oncoming traffic and where vehicles are following one another closely.

Seat Belts

Where seat belts are fitted to the front seats they must be used.

Bikes in Traffic

Amsterdam has at least as many cyclists as motorists. The Dutch treat cyclists with great consideration and drivers usually allow them a much greater safety margin than in other countries. Watch out for junctions with cycle tracks where cyclists often have the right of way.

Parking

No parking is allowed on any of the many canal bridges. Although there are some parking spaces on the edge of the canals they are nearly always occupied. If you do find one, take great care when parking or leaving because there is often nothing to stop you ending up in the water.

Cars parked on pavements are towed away by the Amsterdam police.

Right of Way

Traffic from the right has priority in Amsterdam at all times and this applies even to the smallest sidestreet, which means that drivers should watch out for every single road junction.

Travel Documents

Passports

Visitors from Britain and most Western countries require only a valid passport (or a British Visitor's Passport) to enter the Netherlands.

Driving Licence/
Car Documents

British or other Western driving licences and car documents are accepted in the Netherlands and should accompany the driver.

Green Card

Although nationals of EEC countries do not need an international insurance certificate (green card) it is desirable to have one, otherwise only third-party cover is provided.

Country of Origin

All foreign cars visiting the Netherlands must display an international distinguishing sign of the approved pattern and design showing the country of origin.

Trailers

No customs documents are required if the trailer is clearly being used.

Bicycles and Mopeds

No customs documents required.

Boats

No customs documents required if used for purposes of tourism.

Travelling to Amsterdam

By Car

A number of companies operate ferries between Great Britain and the Netherlands and it is advisable to find out from your travel agent which crossing is the most suitable for your needs. Crossings include:
Sealink ferry from Harwich to Hoek van Holland
North Sea ferries from Hull to Rotterdam
Car ferry service from Sheerness to Flushing
Norfolk Line from Great Yarmouth to Scheveningen
Townsend Thoresen from Felixstowe to Zeebrugge (Belgium)

By Coach

Travel by coach is becoming increasingly popular and Amsterdam is a favourite destination for city tours. Many companies offer a variety of inexpensive tours and there are regular coach services to Amsterdam from London and certain other towns and cities in Britain. Check with your local travel agent.

Practical Information

By Air

There are connections between Amsterdam's main airport, Schiphol, and all major U.S. and European airports. From October 1986 a direct service links the airport to the Centraal Station by rail. The existing bus link is suspended.

By Rail

The main rail service is via the Sealink ferry between Harwich and Hoek van Holland. Further details and reservations are available.

In the UK from:
British Rail
Liverpool Street Station
London EC2. Tel. 01–247 7600

Netherlands Railways
4 New Burlington Street
London SW1. Tel. 01–734 3301

In Amsterdam from:
Nederlands spoorwegen
Stationsplein
Tel. 020 25 51 51

British Rail
Leidseplein 5
Tel. 020 23 41 33

The Central Station in Amsterdam has tourist information centres (VVV), exchange bureaux, taxis, tram and bus connections. Information regarding fares, timetables and overnight accommodation can be obtained from British Rail.

Hotel Reservations

Pre-booking of a hotel room, even in student hotels, can be made through:
Nationaal Reserveringscentrum (NRC)
O.O. Box 404
2260 AK Leidschedam
Tel. 070/20 25 00

Youth Hostels

See Hotels

Important Telephone Numbers at a Glance

Emergency Numbers	Telephone Number
AA (London)	09–44–1–954–7373
Ambulance	22 22 22
Breakdowns (ANWB patrol service)	73 08 44
Counselling Service for alcohol and drugs	23 78 65
Doctor, Dentist, Chemist (medical emergency)	64 21 11
Fire brigade	21 21 21
Police	22 22 22
RAC (London)	09–44–1–686–2525
Airlines	
Air UK	37 02 11
Canadian Pacific	22 44 44
KLM	74 77 47
Pan Am	26 20 21
Qantas	25 50 15
SAA/SAL	16 44 44
Consulates	
Australia	(070) 63 09 83
Canada	(070) 61 41 11
South Africa	(070) 92 45 01
United Kingdom	73 61 28
United States of America	79 03 21
Hospitals	
Academisch Medisch Centrum	5 66 91 11
V.U. Ziekenhuis	5 48 91 11
Lucas Ziekenhuis	5 10 89 11
Onze Lieve Vrouwe Gasthuis	5 99 91 11
Ziekenhuis Amsterdam-Noord	36 89 22
Information	
Airport	5 11 04 32
GVB (public transport undertaking)	27 27 27
Railway station	23 83 83
Tourist offices	
VVV (tourist information centres)	26 64 44
Netherlands National Tourist Offices	
Johannesburg	09 27 11 23 69 91
London	09 44 1 499 9367/8/9/0
New York	09 1 (212) 245–5320
San Francisco	09 1 (415) 781–3387
Sydney	09 61 2 27 69 21
Toronto	09 1 (416) 598–2830/2831
Vancouver	09 1 (604) 684–5720
Lost Property	5 99 25 50

Taxis	77 77 77

Telephoning

Information (international calls)	00 18
Operator connected calls	00 10
Dialling codes:	
To Australia	09 61
To Canada	09 1
To South Africa	09 27
To United Kingdom	09 44
To United States of America	09 1
From United Kingdom to Amsterdam	010 31 20

Notes

Notes

Notes